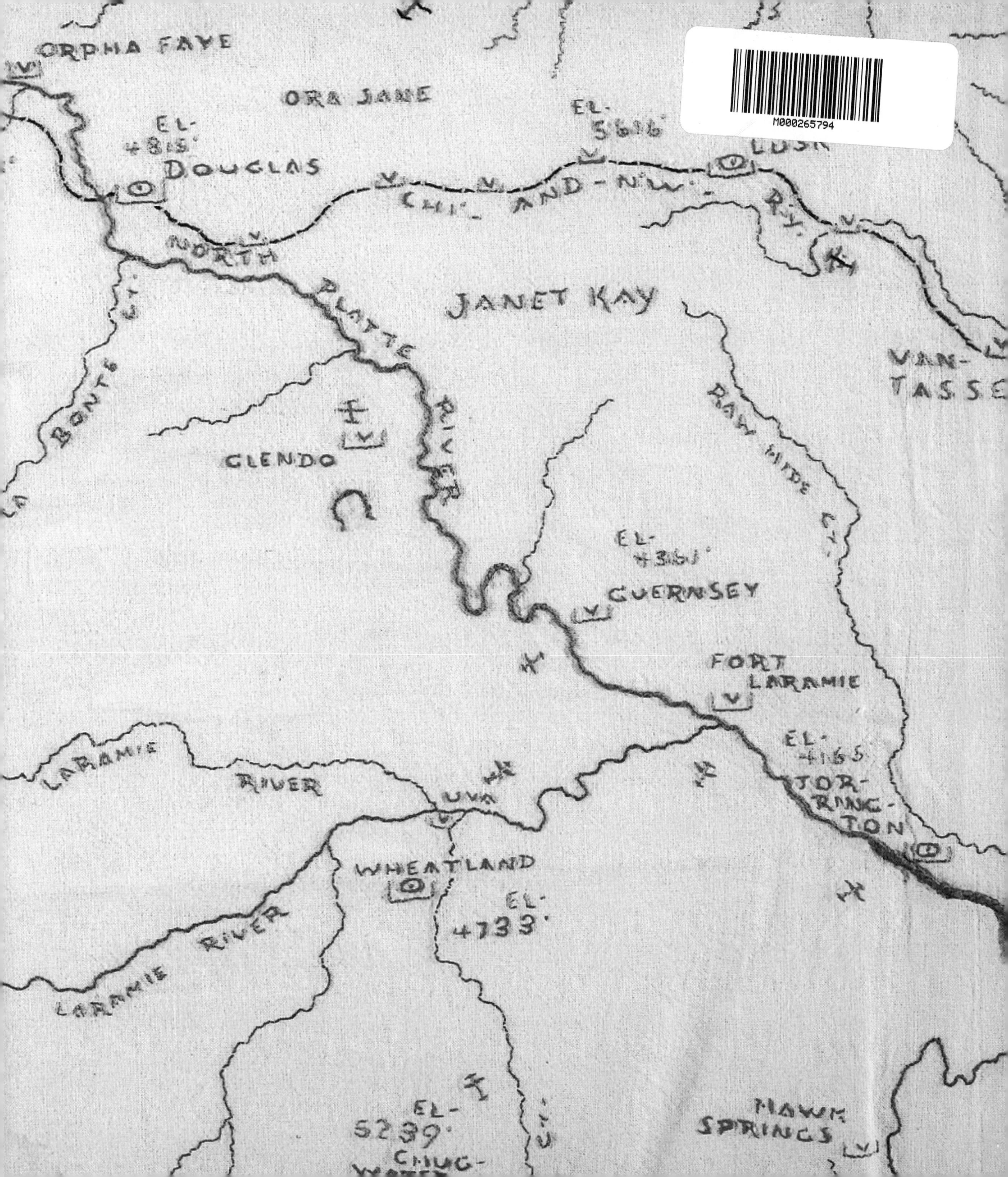
ORPHA FAYE
ORA JANE
EL-
4815'
DOUGLAS
EL-
5616'
LUSK
CHI. AND-N.W.-RY.
NORTH
PLATTE
RIVER
JANET KAY
BONTE CR.
GLENDO
RAW HIDE CR.
VAN-
TASSE
EL-
4361'
GUERNSEY
FORT
LARAMIE
EL-
4165'
TOR-
RING-
TON
LARAMIE
RIVER
UVA
WHEATLAND
EL-
4733'
LARAMIE RIVER
HAWK
SPRINGS
EL-
5239'
CHUG-

GOING WEST! QUILTS AND COMMUNITY

Introduction by RODERICK KIRACOFE

with contributions by SANDI FOX

Going West!

QUILTS AND COMMUNITY

SMITHSONIAN AMERICAN ART MUSEUM, Washington, D.C., in association with D GILES, LIMITED, London

The Smithsonian American Art Museum
gratefully acknowledges the generous support of
HELEN AND PETER BING
for this publication of
Going West! Quilts and Community
and the accompanying exhibition.
The exhibition is presented at the
Museum's Renwick Gallery from
October 5, 2007 through January 21, 2008.

Designed by Carol Beehler

Library of Congress Cataloging-in-Publication Data
Going West! : quilts and community / introduction by Roderick Kiracofe ; with contributions by Sandi Fox.
    p. cm.
    Accompanies an exhibition at the Renwick Gallery, Washington, D.C., Oct. 5, 2007–Jan. 21, 2008.
    Includes bibliographical references.
    ISBN 978-1-904832-45-4 (hardcover : alk. paper)
    1. Quilts—Nebraska—History—19th century—Exhibitions. 2. Quilts—Nebraska—History—20th century—Exhibitions. 3. Frontier and pioneer life—West (U.S.)—Exhibitions. I. Kiracofe, Roderick. II. Fox, Sandi. III. Renwick Gallery. IV. Smithsonian American Art Museum.

NK9112.G65 2007
746.4609782′074753—dc22

                    2007020702

Printed and bound in Italy on acid-free paper.

The Smithsonian American Art Museum is home to one of the largest collections of American art in the world. Its holdings—more than 41,000—tell the story of America through the visual arts and represent the most inclusive collection of American art of any museum today. It is the nation's first federal art collection, predating the 1846 founding of the Smithsonian Institution. The Museum celebrates the exceptional creativity of the nation's artist whose insights into history, society, and the individual reveal the essence of the American experience.

The Renwick Gallery, SAAM's satellite museum, collects and displays American crafts and decorative arts from the nineteenth to the twenty-first centuries, and is located on Pennsylvania Avenue at 17th Street NW.

For more information or a catalogue of publications, write: Office of Publications, Smithsonian American Art Museum, MRC 970, PO Box 37012, Washington, D.C. 20013-7012.

Visit the Museum's Web site at **AmericanArt.si.edu**.

Cover: *Mary Brown Elliot's Sunburst Quilt*, dated 1837 (detail). See p. 18.
Endpapers: *Pieced, Appliquéd, and Embroidered Map Panel* (showing the state of Nebraska), about 1930 (detail). See pp. 120–21.
Title page: *Pieced Quilt, Concentric Strips and Triangles*, about 1875 (detail). See p. 60.

Credits
Unless otherwise noted, all photographs are reproduced courtesy of the lenders. Photography by Gene Young, except the following: cover images and pages 6 (bottom), 25, 44–49, 69, 88–89, 98–99, and 112–13 by Steven Oliver. Page 11: art © Robert Rauschenberg/Licensed by VAGA, NY; digital image © The Museum of Modern Art/Licensed by SCALA/Art Resource, NY; p. 34: courtesy Missouri Historical Society, St. Louis.

Author Sandi Fox gratefully acknowledges the Nebraska State Quilt Guild, whose development and funding of their Quilt Preservation Project created her interest in Nebraska's quilts.

Smithsonian American Art Museum

D Giles Limited
2nd Floor
162-164 Upper Richmond Road
London SW15 2SL
United Kingdom

Contents

America's Abstract Art

ELIZABETH BROUN

AMERICA'S first abstract artists were the native Indians who used dyed quills and earth ochres to order their world and ornament themselves and their most sacred objects. After the Indians came the quiltmakers. In colonial and early Federal America, merchants imported expensive, richly printed calicoes and chintzes from Europe that women made into high-style bedcovers, turning provincial rooms into art galleries of dazzling display. Americans developed their own printing technologies in the 1840s and began making elaborately patterned textiles at low cost. The bedcover "industry" was quickly democratized as women and young girls everywhere picked up needle and thread and small cloth leftovers to create their own quilts. Some featured a flower basket or an urn in the center of their quilts, but most used their abundant ingenuity to create purely abstract patterns from pieced fabric scraps. Quilt patterns have proliferated over two centuries, each seemingly more ingenious than the last, and quiltmaking remains a popular art form today for many women and an increasing number of men. A quick Internet search shows that there are more than one thousand Web sites offering thousands of free patterns to today's ever-inventive quilters.

Browsing traditional quilt patterns is a quick way to grasp how intimately this art form is connected to the American frontier experience. Millwheel, Crossing Ohio, Virginia Reel, Arrowshead, Indian Trail, Bear's Paw, Shoo-fly, 54-40 or Fight, Log Cabin, Square Dance, Accordions, Churn Dash, and hundreds more speak to our country's pre-industrial past. Flying Geese, Flying Fish, Spider's Den, Maple Leaf, Sunrise Star, Blazing Star, Night and Day, Milky Way, Stepping Stones, Thistle Bloom, and countless more tell that Americans used to live on more intimate terms

All measurements are given in inches, height x width, followed by centimeters in parentheses.

Log Cabin, "Barn Raising" Variation, 1882 (detail). See p. 64.

with nature. And of course there are "formalists" in every abstract movement, so we find also four-patch, five-patch, nine-patch, twenty-five-patch, All Those Squares!, Square in Square, Chevron, Chain, Braid, X's and O's, Cat's Cradle, Balkan Puzzle, ZigZag, and so many more. Just reciting the names is a kind of joyful poetry.

The urge to fill a big visual field with color patterns is universal, though less valued in Western societies today than in centuries past. Throughout history, abstraction gained urgency and meaning whenever a culture banned imagery and icons from its own religious art. This phenomenon of iconoclasm recurs regularly throughout history—in the Roman Empire, Islamic cultures, the Eastern Orthodox Church, and the Russian Revolution. It occurred most recently in America's modern art—our secular religion—in the 1950s and 1960s, when critic Clement Greenberg banned representation and narration and all "external" meaning from the work of the Color Field painters whom he advised. In more tolerant eras, when representation and narration are permitted and encouraged, color patterning may fall back to the borders of the image, or retreat still further into the functional arts of ceramics and fabric design. But this eternal desire, even need, to create color patterns and abstract designs springs from the same impulses across the ages—psychology, sensuality, revolution, mathematics, physics, discipline, order, and spirituality. Pattern and color are infinitely variable and reveal the lines and shapes of thought itself. They are the record of mental activity, revealed through the senses. Whether in the form of East Indian mandalas or American Indian sandpaintings, abstract color designs are a symbolic representation of the cosmos.

So why are Shaker quilts called "craft" or "functional design," while Kasimir Malevich paintings and Kenneth Noland paintings are "high art"? Some might say it's about the intentionality of the artist or the depth of the underlying philosophy that inspired the artwork. Others might say it's just the usual art-world politics, which relegates women's work to non-art status. One curiosity is that we tend today to regard abstraction as a time-bound movement rather than as an ever-present expression of human thought. The abstract impulse has become disassociated from its vast body of antecedents in every culture, so it now self-identifies as something "modern" that is ever being affirmed as "new." The April 2007 ARTnews is celebrating "The New Abstraction," and an exhibition at the DeCordova Museum in Lincoln, Massachusetts ("Big Bang! Abstract Painting for the 21st Century") claims that the inspiration for today's "New Abstraction" comes from "computer technology, cosmology, quantum physics, information theory, genetics, complexity theory, remote sensing, and other sets of current scientific visual languages," which sounds both very new and very male. Critics agree that the "New Abstraction" is absolutely not about decoration, which is understood to be both old and female. According to Linda Norden, independent curator, "The problem with abstraction is always its closeness to the decorative, to something that feels escapist and closed-eyed rather than probing."

Even as the art world strains to separate "art" sheep from "decoration" goats, it's good to remember those who subvert the categories. Robert Rauschenberg's 1955 combine painting called *Bed* is high art by anyone's standard, though it is ironically celebrated for its closeness to the vernacular (fig. 1). Expressionist brushwork animates the upper half, while the lower half is a pieced bed quilt in the "Courthouse Steps" pattern. (And so Rauschenberg gives visual clarity to the idea of "high" and "low" art.) The Museum of Modern Art label for *Bed* says, "Legend has it that the bedclothes are Rauschenberg's own," and notes that this makes the work a kind of self-portrait. It says that by hanging on the wall, *Bed* "loses its function, but not its associations with sleep, dreams, illness, sex—the most intimate moments in life." The label neglects the quilt as an expressive artwork in its own right, with complex meanings that Rauschenberg has appropriated for his own purposes. It assumes that the quilt's meaning derives purely from its personal connection to the artist.

Even if the label-writer cannot see it, surely the deeply rooted Rauschenberg knew that those "most intimate moments in life" would not have been evoked as well by any other kind of bedcovering. Quilts resonate with life associations—the exciting optical dazzle and creativity of their makers; their endless improvisation on geometry and nature; the labor and love of the mothers, aunts, sisters, and daughters who made them; their many uses and re-uses, and their power as objects of intense physical materiality. The current debate about art and decoration would find no place in the larger sphere of world art across time; it reflects rather the limited scope of our own narrower conversations today. So this volume celebrates those early abstract quilters who—before Kandinsky and the Stieglitz Circle modernists—used abstraction to such profound effect. Fortunately these quiltmakers were not dissuaded by allegations of "decoration" from cherishing their creations as prized possessions, to be taken on the long journey west and treasured for posterity, that is, for us. Though many quiltmakers are anonymous, they stand—and stand out—in a very long tradition of great artists who use color patterns to reveal our world. ✹

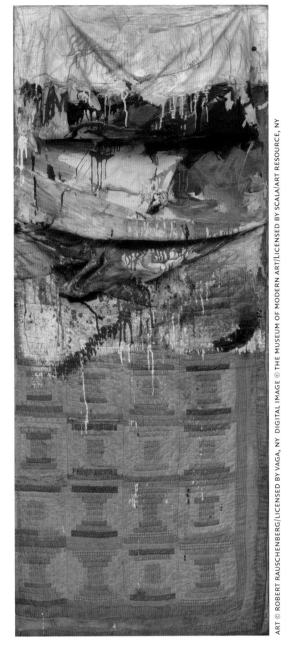

Fig. 1 Robert Rauschenberg, *Bed*, 1955, combine painting: oil and pencil on pillow, quilt and sheet on wood supports, 75 ¼ x 31 ½ x 8 (191.1 x 80 x 20.3). The Museum of Modern Art, Gift of Leo Castelli in honor of Alfred H. Barr, Jr.

Acknowledgments

ONCE UPON A TIME, I was talking with a good friend, Helen Bing, about how much I love the dazzling pieced quilts that I used to see throughout my Kansas childhood. They were part of the common culture there, and I miss them after living so long in Washington, D.C. I knew that Helen would understand. She was raised in Minnesota, where quilts are also part of the "fabric of life," though for a long time she has lived in California, so she too feels the tug of an earlier experience in a very different place. Kansas and Minnesota and all the north-central plains experience long frigid winters, so the nineteenth-century quilting tradition was naturally strong there, leaving a rich legacy of amazing textiles that have been passed down through families for generations and stored in old trunks, to surface again in antique stores and flea markets. They are part nostalgia, part "collectible," and part inspiration. It's fun to see how quilting is alive and well today, not just in rural farming communities, but among professional women too, in Kansas City and Omaha and Milwaukee.

Helen Bing told me about Sandi Fox, an independent curator in Los Angeles who had created some wonderful quilt exhibitions and catalogues. I asked Sandi to think about a theme for another quilt show, and she came up with the idea of highlighting the wonderful quilts that have accumulated over decades in Nebraska, which was the destination of many early settlers who used the Great Platte River trail. Sandi had already done considerable research in Nebraska institutions, which had extensive records created by the Nebraska State Quilt Guild, which created the Quilt Preservation Project there. And so this exhibition and catalogue were conceived. Helen Bing loved hearing about these plans, and generously offered to support the project.

The Renwick Gallery is a branch of the Smithsonian American Art Museum devoted to contemporary crafts and their historical decorative arts antecedents. The Renwick had featured wonderful quilt shows in the 1990s. But since its founding in 1972, the Renwick has never presented an exhibition of classic nineteenth-century pieced quilts, which are complex material objects with a wealth of "embedded" cultural meaning. This exhibition, then, is a first for this premier museum devoted to craft traditions.

We especially thank the lenders for their generous spirit and for their expertise about these collections. They provided access to Sandi Fox for research and they agreed to extended loans that allowed the Museum to complete photography for the catalogue well in advance of the exhibition. A complete list of lenders is on pages 14–15. As preservationists, caretakers, scholars, enthusiasts, and incredible sources of information, the staff of these museums and historical societies deserve our thanks.

The stories of the quilts and objects in the exhibition are often lore that was initially preserved by a family, a church, or a small community. We are grateful to Rex Wagner of the Shieldstrom family for having shared his family's story; to Carol A. Sisco, editor of the *Pawnee Republican* for her search of the paper's archives; and to David Wells, historian of the Grand Army of the Republic. We also thank Kevin Jones of the Fashion Institute of Design and Merchandising and Sharon Shore of Caring for Textiles, both of Los Angeles, for sharing their expertise on nineteenth-century dressmaking and sewing techniques.

Among the many institutions that provided essential access for research are the Nebraska State Historical Society at Lincoln; the Missouri Historical Society, St. Louis; Church Archives of the Church of Jesus Christ of Latter-day Saints, Salt Lake City, Utah; Lane County Historical Society, Oregon; Digital Library and Archives, University Libraries, Virginia Polytechnic Institute and State University, Blacksburg; and the Historical Society of Douglas County, Library/Archives Center at Omaha.

We are grateful to Steven Oliver for his exquisite photography of the quilts and objects. His care with these fragile objects and his appreciation of their beauty allows every reader to see them in their full glory and in exquisite detail. And we thank Shelly Kale, whose patient reading of the manuscript and research files ensured accuracy in the myriad details of a complex project. And we are deeply grateful for all the efforts of our talented and dedicated colleagues at the Smithsonian American Art Museum and our Renwick Gallery for their superb contributions to this exhibition and book.

As is the case in so many of the quilts documented here, many hands have joined together to make this exhibition and book a pleasing whole. ✹

ELIZABETH BROUN
The Margaret and Terry Stent Director
Smithsonian American Art Museum
May 2007

Lenders

Grateful acknowledgment is made to the following collections, all in the state of Nebraska, for their participation in the exhibition and catalogue.

Burt County Museum, *Tekamah*

Cherry County Historical Museum, *Valentine*

Clay County Museum, *Clay Center*

Custer County Historical Society, *Broken Bow*

Dawson County Historical Society Museum, *Lexington*

Douglas County Historical Society, General Crook House Museum, *Omaha*

Durham Western Heritage Museum, *Omaha*

Fairbury City Museum

Fort Sidney Museum, *Sidney*

Gage County Historical Society Museum, *Beatrice*

Hastings Museum of Natural and Cultural History

High Plains Historical Museum, *McCook*

Historical Society of Garden County, *Oshkosh*

Holt County Historical Society, *O'Neill*

Howells Historical Society Museum

International Quilt Study Center, University of Nebraska-Lincoln

Loup County Historical Society, *Taylor*

Merrick County Historical Museum, *Central City*

Nebraska Prairie Museum of the Phelps County Historical Society, *Holdrege*

Nebraska State Historical Society, *Lincoln*

North Platte Valley Museum, *Gering*

Anna Bemis Palmer Museum, *York*

Pawnee City Historical Society and Museum

Plains Historical Society, *Kimball*

Plainsman Museum, *Aurora*

Rock County Historical Society Museum, *Bassett*

Sarpy County Historical Museum, *Bellevue*

Stuart White Horse Museum

Stuhr Museum of the Prairie Pioneer, *Grand Island*

Washington County Historical Association, *Fort Calhoun*

Webster County Historical Museum, *Red Cloud*

Introduction

RODERICK KIRACOFE

A QUILT IS VIRTUAL HISTORY. When it was made, where, and why, and then what happened next echo the arc of both profound national events and intimate private lives.

The quilts in *Going West* offer many fascinating stories. Their when, where, and why are very different. It's the "what happened next" that unites them. As in an intricately crafted novel where all the characters suddenly converge, each of these well-traveled quilts ended up in the same place, however much their owners intended otherwise. Each arrived at the geographical center of the United States and remained there, gathered now from collections and archives in the state of Nebraska.

So many books have been written about quilts, so many exhibitions mounted. Why are we so interested in and deeply touched by quilts? Why, when the industrial age and urbanization made them unnecessary and even unfashionable, have they continued to endure and inspire? What stories and connections do we each have to quilts? How do we look at them, and why do we stand in awe before each of the objects in this exhibit? What do they say to us?

Going West! Quilts and Community presents more than fifty stories in cloth. Sandi Fox has traced and woven a rich and moving history of the lives and hands that created the objects presented within these pages. Some of these stories are intensely personal. Others illustrate the power and influence of the community, of political, economic, and social movements, and of national pride. Some are funny, some tragic; all are inspirational. Each story tells us something about the great westerly migration of the nineteenth and early twentieth centuries—from Europe to North

Rebecca Ellen Slyh's Quilt, dated 1852 (detail).
See p. 19.

America, from the New World's eastern coast to the central and western continent. Millions of people, the largest voluntary migration in the history of our planet, formed a flood of humanity, mingling and merging their cultural and artistic heritages.

Starting in the 1840s, three of the major trails to the western United States paralleled each other along the Great Platte River, through what is now Nebraska. The Oregon Trail, the Mormon Trail, and the California Trail converged, carrying wagon trains and settlers bound for farther west. Some at this point decided they'd gone as far as they could or would on the perilous journey. They stayed and turned the Great American Desert into farmland.[1] In the 1860s, Nebraska became a destination in itself, with homesteaders competing for free land granted by the federal government and later lured to land offered by the railroad companies.

Whether the *Going West* quilts arrived in Nebraska by covered wagon or, later, via the railroad, most represented an intense connection with "back home," a place that the traveler was unlikely ever to see again. This was usually, as Sandi Fox points out, "a journey that promised no return."[2] Most of the bedding for such a journey was utilitarian, but even a well-worn old quilt or a new one autographed by friends and family provided a supportive connection with those left behind. Such quilts brought joy and comfort to those who slept under them. And among the practical goods might be a treasured master quilt, one of those superb examples of needlework that had taken a thousand skilled hours or more to create. This quilt now promised that the new life might someday provide the same level of civility as the old—if not better. Although most travelers dreamed of prosperity, land, and a fine new house worthy of displaying such a treasure, it appears that some women went reluctantly. The sense of adventure and exploration belonged primarily to the men, and many women saw little in the journey but hardships. When the hardships and horrors of the trail seemed overwhelming, such a quilt could be lifted from an old chest to touch, feel, and smell, invoking consoling memories.

Fig. 1 Mary Brown Elliot, *Mary Brown Elliot's Sunburst Quilt*, provenance unknown, dated 1837, cotton; pieced and quilted, 95¾ x 95 (243.2 x 241.3). Washington County Historical Association, Fort Calhoun

Fig. 2 Rebecca Ellen Slyh, *Rebecca Ellen Slyh's Quilt*, Franklin County, Ohio, dated 1852, cotton; pieced, appliquéd, quilted, corded and stuffed, and embroidered, 98 x 81 (248 x 207). International Quilt Study Center, University of Nebraska-Lincoln, 1997.009.0001

Two of the earliest quilts in *Going West* are examples of such masterworks: *Mary Brown Elliot's Sunburst Quilt*, dated 1837 (fig. 1), and *Rebecca Ellen Slyh's Quilt* from Ohio, dated 1852 (fig. 2). It was an act of faith even to commit such treasures to an uncertain fate. How many such quilts started the perilous expedition and had to be discarded beside the trail along with other possessions to lighten the load as wagons broke down and horses and oxen died? When loved ones died, a quilt might be wrapped around them before they were left behind in a shallow grave in the wilderness, a final act of love amid the unbearable sadness.

WHAT IS A QUILT?

The word *quilt* is a technical term that has expanded to mean many things to many people. To some, a quilt is a big, thick blanket that goes on a bed, a symbol of comfort, safety, and all that was good about the past. To others, it is something that hangs on the wall of an art gallery or home, exciting, vibrant, modern. Disputes arise about whether quilting is an "art" or a "craft," whether the word *craft* is simply a derogatory way of defining art done by women. Debates rage about political correctness, sexism, and the value placed on women's work. The simple word *quilt* has become laden with connotations—emotional, political, psychological, and economic.

Specifically, the word refers to two or more layers of fabric that are sewn or tied together, usually with a filling. "Quilting" refers to the stitches that hold the sandwich layers together. The term *quilt* is not technically limited to a bedcover. Quilted garments have been found in ancient Egyptian and Chinese tombs. Customarily, there is a filling between the fabric layers of quilted American bedcoverings, most commonly wool, cotton, or feathers, but survival quilts have been stuffed with whatever was at hand, including rags, pine needles, corn husks, newspapers, or dried leaves.

When a traditional bed quilt was washed, the wool or cotton batting inside tended to shift and wad up into small balls. (In fact, what Americans call quilt batting is referred to as wadding in Great Britain.) This internal shifting could be prevented by a great deal of stitching, creating spaces as small as two inches apart or less. While a simple grid of stitches would do the trick, the necessity inspired the creation of elaborate stitching designs. In Europe, where "whole-cloth" quilts were the norm, the stitching alone provided the surface design, as in the beautiful *Swedish Red Silk Quilt* (see p. 36).

Although Europeans sometimes used piecework, also called patchwork— stitching small pieces of different-colored cloth into patterns—the technique positively flourished in North America. This is often ascribed to the limited supplies of textiles available to the earliest settlers, which was generally not the case. Nevertheless, fabric was often precious, either handwoven or imported at great cost, so scraps were cherished and recycled. However, once economical, commercially woven fabrics were readily available, the craft became more popular than ever. Obviously, quiltmaking served another invaluable purpose besides warmth. It allowed the makers an outlet for individual artistic expression and creativity.

Today, polyester batting no longer requires close stitching, but many quilters continue the traditions of intricate quilting. Commercial blankets make quilted bedcovers obsolete, yet the art and craft of quilting enjoys enormous popularity and has for two hundred years. Recognition of needlework as fiber art has even raised new quandaries for quilt shows and competitions: defining "what is a quilt?" Are structures assembled from layered aluminum cans, postage stamps, or dryer lint encased in clear plastic actually "quilts"? Some say, "Yes, of course." Some say an equally resounding, "No!" It is an ongoing, intriguing, and irresolvable debate akin to the question, what is art?

The quilts you are about to meet, however, require no semantic debate. They are pure history-on-the-hoof, created from a desire to warm the body and also the heart. They are inseparable from the lives of their makers and users, a chronicle of passions, joys, grief, frustrations, and hopes. What do these quilts have to tell us?

COMPARE AND CONTRAST

The quilts presented here offer some dynamic contrasts. There's the finely appliquéd and intricately quilted *"Prince's Feathers" Quilt* from Preble County, Ohio (see p. 52), where my paternal grandmother reared her eleven children and stitched her quilts. Such a quilt was probably displayed on the bed in the guest room, actually slept under only by the most honored visitor. Compare this with the humble, well-loved doll quilt (see p. 67) that comforted a child during the dangerous journey west. Its maker and exact history are unknown. Did it survive, despite its tattered condition, because the child also survived and kept it into adulthood as a memento of a life-changing adventure? Or was its owner one of the thousands who never completed the journey, another statistic of the western migration, and the quilt subsequently cherished by the bereaved mother as a tangible memory of her lost child?

Two quilts using embroidered words offer another alpha–omega contrast. The *Omaha Commerce Quilt* (see p. 76) shows how quilting could involve an entire community. The piece is a group effort, a fund-raising quilt made by the members of the Ladies Aid Society of the Grace Evangelical Lutheran Church in Omaha. Local businesses "purchased" advertising space on its surface, each design drafted and stitched by a different woman—which is obvious from the varying levels of skill. (The forty-two subscribers include two undertaking establishments! A commentary on the high mortality rate of the time?) The resulting quilt was undoubtedly displayed, thus providing mini-billboard publicity for the donating commercial enterprises. Afterward, it might have been either auctioned or raffled to raise additional funds or presented to a civic leader.

The *Omaha Commerce Quilt* was an expansion of a popular if somewhat less ambitious fund-raising technique commonly used in the late nineteenth and early twentieth centuries. Local people would pay five, ten, or twenty-five cents to sign their

Fig. 3 Edith Withers Meyers, *You are the Darling
of the Earth Crazy Quilt*, about 1898, wool,
76 x 65 (193 x 165.1). Nebraska State Historical
Society, Lincoln

Fig. 4 *You are the Darling of the Earth*, about 1898
(detail).

names on a quilt block, then the signatures were stitched over by the members of the
fund-raising group, "immortalizing" the donor. Often there was a key block indicat-
ing the cause for which money was being raised. Occasionally, the winner of the auction or raffle would then donate the quilt back to be raffled again, raising even more
money for the cause. Such quilts became especially popular during the Civil War to
support widows and provide the troops on both sides with much-needed supplies.

Contrast the community-wide involvement of these group quilts with the
intensely personal "diary" of the heavily embroidered crazy quilt by Edith Withers
Meyers called *You are the Darling of the Earth* (fig. 3). Rather than committing her life to

the pages of a traditional journal, this exuberant maker has chronicled important events, the names of her friends, and even contemporary slang in running-stitch script on cloth. It is fascinating to speculate why she chose this more labor-intensive medium. She must have been young at the time, with a lively social life—her inscriptions hint that she was not yet married and focused on husband and children. The dates in the inscriptions are 1898, and she commemorates the kind of occasions so important to youth like the "skating party on North River" and the "Swede Dance." She delights in memorializing the latest slang like "Toots" and "Buzz" and "Yes, you bet." There is even a sly reference—to a rival in love or a disapproving relative?—stating, "Ada was mad." Finally, a block is somewhat enigmatically inscribed "done at lass," or more likely "done at last" (fig. 4). Were these the final stitches of her labors and, in her haste, she forgot to cross the t? Try to imagine the high-spirited creator of this unique chronicle of life in turn-of-the-century Nebraska.

Contemplate the sweetly innocent and somewhat abstract cross-stitched "drawing" of the repeated pots of flowers against the multicolored wool panels of the *Embroidered Wool Bedcover* (see p. 110). This was made by a twelve-year-old girl, probably using outdated wool samples discarded by a dressmaker or tailor. Such sturdy, useful fabric came precut in identical rectangles. It would be far too good to waste, but how to feminize and individualize it? Notice the placement of the colored wool panels, the pink center, and the carefully thought-out arrangement of her other colors (fig. 5). Were flowers simply a conventional decorative choice, or was she demonstrating the importance of the garden and plant life to women in the nineteenth and twentieth centuries? Striking a balance between the practical and the artistic was an ongoing struggle, and if a task could encompass both, so much the better. In the garden, rows were arranged with a pleasing sense of order, purpose, and beauty. So were their quilts.

A plain-and-fancy contrast to this embroidered quilt is provided by a similar but unadorned quilt, also constructed of various sizes of wool samples. Such a quilt was probably made by a mother for a son or other male family member (fig. 6).

Fig. 5 Mrs. Ken Armbruster, *Embroidered Wool Bedcover*, 1904 (detail). See p. 110.

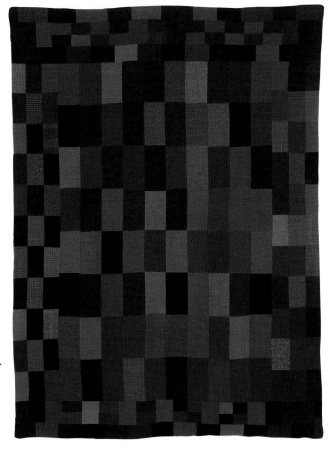

Fig. 6 Unidentified maker, *Men's Suit Samples (Quilt) Comforter*, about 1902, wool, 85½ x 65 (217.2 x 165.1). Stuhr Museum of the Prairie Pioneer, Grand Island

THE MESSAGE IS THE MEDIUM

The quilts in *Going West* exist as a form of personal expression. They recall a brave, genuinely creative spirit. Those women who signed, initialed, or dated their work in thread left traces of themselves deeply imprinted within the fabric.

Although the vast majority of quilts convey their messages through imagery alone, an impressive number of quilts in *Going West* offer actual words. Someone took needle and thread to inscribe specific messages and record names. Indeed, in one of my personal favorites, created by Swedish Methodist Church members, the thirty-six blue stars that spangle the surface consist *entirely* of names (fig. 7). Compare this to the more traditional "signature block" quilt for which the signatures were incorporated into a common pieced-block pattern (fig. 8).

The mid-nineteenth century experienced a rise in romanticism and an increase in literacy that made autograph collecting popular. The development of inks

Fig. 7 Swedish Methodist Church members, *Blue Embroidered Spokes of Signatures*, 1926, cotton, 81 ½ x 80 (207 x 203.2). Nebraska Prairie Museum of the Phelps County Historical Society, Holdrege

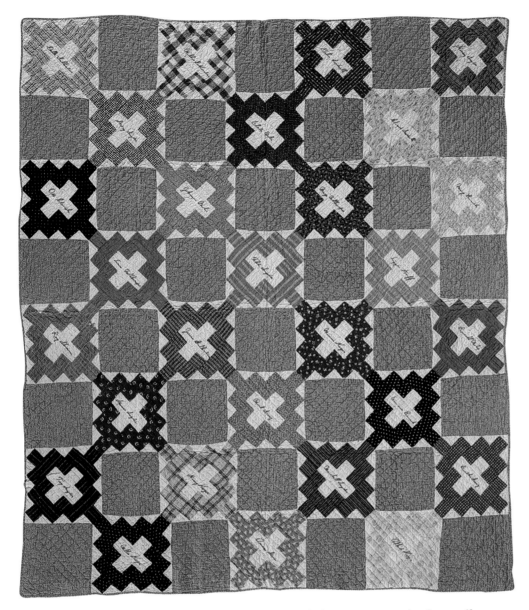

thought to be permanent to cloth soon extended the custom to signing quilts, though the "signature quilts" or "autograph quilts" that have survived best tend to have their inked autographs gone over in outline stitching. Inked writing and motifs have been found on quilts dating from 1830, with full-fledged signature quilts appearing as early as 1839.[3]

Besides the communal fund-raising efforts already discussed, many friendship, commemorative, or presentation quilts were created for individuals. This might have been on the occasion of a marriage, but usually signified that the recipient was leaving the community. Separate blocks would be signed by their individual makers and then assembled into a top that was quilted by the group. If a popular teacher or minister was being transferred to a new assignment, many townspeople

Fig. 9 Mrs. Ella Hughes Burke, *Friend Ship Quilt, started in 1898 & finished 1928*, 1931, cotton, 84 x 67 (213.4 x 170.2). Fort Sidney Museum, Sidney

Fig. 9 Mrs. Ella Hughes Burke, *Friend Ship Quilt, started in 1898 & finished 1928*, 1931, cotton, 84 x 67 (213.4 x 170.2). Fort Sidney Museum, Sidney

OPPOSITE: Fig. 10 Ellen Holen, *The Holen Boys Ties Quilt*, about 1935, silk, 94 x 81 (238.8 x 205.7). Nebraska Prairie Museum of the Phelps County Historical Society, Holdrege, NE, with permission by the Holen Family

might sign the blocks. These quilts then became mementos of those left behind. The lucky recipient of the handsome blue and white *Friend Ship Quilt* must have been well liked, for the quilt contains 192 signatures, each enclosed in a "petal" of a flower (fig. 9). These circular flower shapes also suggest another recurring theme in *Going West* quilts—the ubiquitous wagon wheel.

Of the many "message" quilts in this exhibition, the one I am most fond of is the one with the most striking visual statement and the simplest embroidered mes-

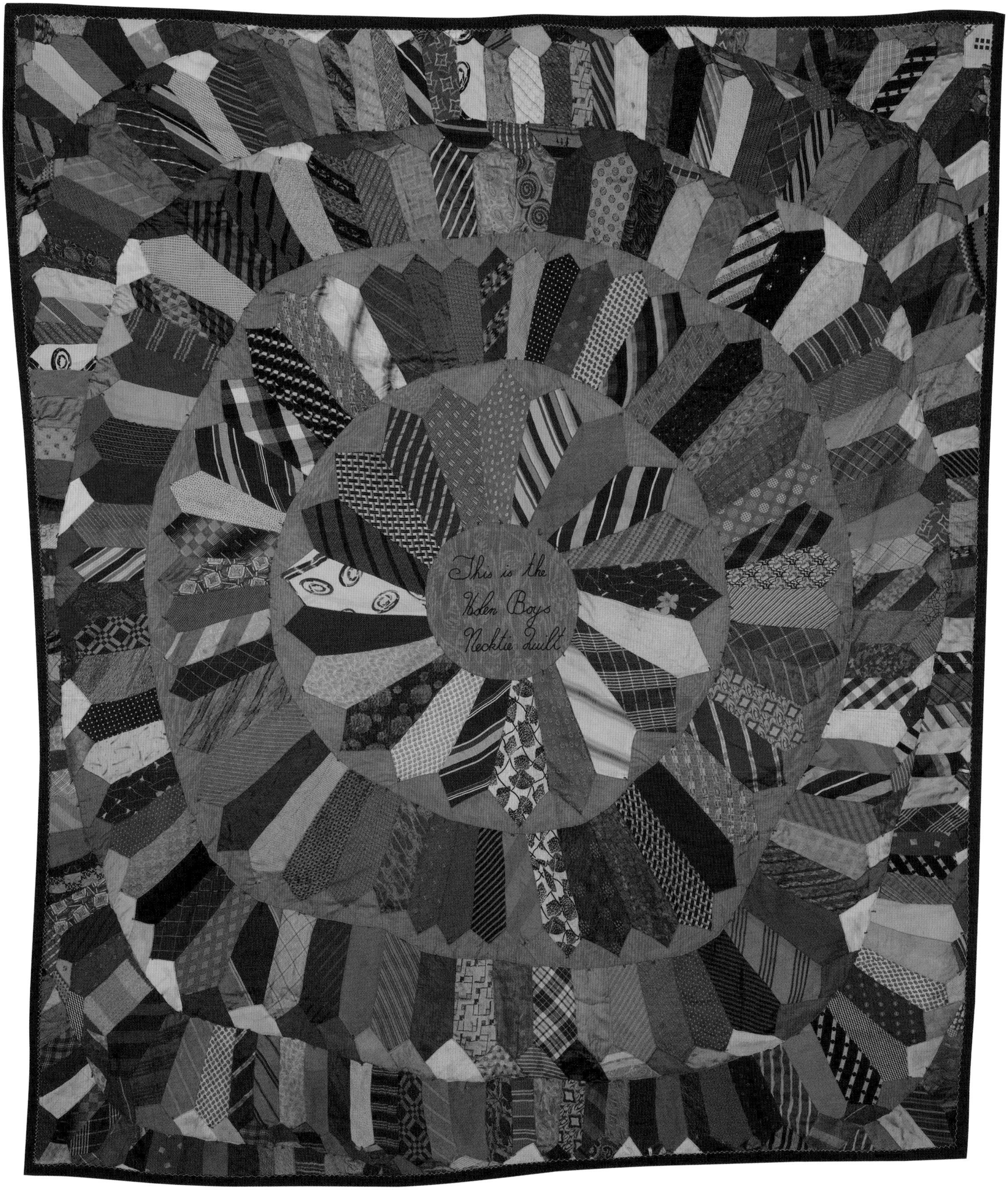
This is the
Holen Boys
Necktie Quilt

sage: "This is the Holen Boys Necktie Quilt" (fig. 10). Nearly a hundred silk neckties explode in a fireball of energy. Who were the Holen boys? How did they have so many neckties, and why did they surrender them for this quilt?

WHEELS WITHIN WHEELS

One recurrent image of the trek west was the spoked circle, seen as representing a wagon wheel. This ancient motif inspired many nineteenth-century quilts and evolved into still popular patterns like the "Dresden Plate" and the many fan variations.

The segmented circle has been a popular symbol since the Stone Age, employed by virtually all cultures in art, religion, mathematics, astrology, astronomy, and science. More than three thousand years ago, the people of India and Sumeria had divided the circle into the 360 degrees we still use today. Druids, Aztecs, and Egyptians used the circle as a mystical symbol of creation or perfection. Even cultures that had not yet "invented" the wheel for transportation (and, therefore, the wagon) employed the spoked circle in their imagery.

My favorite among *Going West's* four examples of wagon-wheel quilts is the dazzling *Wagon Wheels Crazy Quilt* (see p. 70). What memories its creator, Sara Boldon, must have had of the long months on the trail from Indiana. By the turn of the nineteenth century, most crazy quilts were strictly ornamental, fashioned of delicate silks and velvets by ladies of leisure to decorate their drawing rooms. This sturdy woolen construction was most likely intended for a bed, yet even with nine children, Sara found time to embellish the four huge wheels with many decorative stitches, creating an unforgettable work of art.

LOOKING AT VOICES

Besides the questions that quilts raise for me and that I have posed here, what speaks to me the most about the quilts in *Going West* are the threads added to the surface of so many of these quilts in the form of embroidery, names, flowers, buildings, advertisements, and phrases. They provide us with a tangible, vivid link to the lives of their makers.

Why did these people pick up and move west? What called them? What kept them going along the treacherous and difficult journey? What brought them joy? What made them laugh? What caused them to stop and put down roots in this or that place? Where to stop or when to keep going? What was it like for those living in Nebraska to have throngs of people and families passing through as they were putting down roots? What symbols and messages do these quilts convey?

This is not a scientific sampling or a precise account or even a representation of all the quilts brought to or made in Nebraska. This is a very personal gathering, a personal view. Stand and look or sit with these pages and become lost in the mysteries of these quilts, their stories, known and unknown. Allow yourself to be curious about the lives of the people who created and lived with these quilts. Let their voices speak to you through what you see. ✹

1. D. W. Meinig, *The Shaping of America: A Geographical Perspective on 500 Years of History*, vol. 2, *Continental America, 1800–1867* (New Haven: Yale University Press, 1995), 76.

2. Catherine Scott Coburn, quoted in the *Morning Oregonian*, June 17, 1890, in Kenneth L. Holmes, ed., *Covered Wagon Women: Diaries & Letters from the Western Trails, 1840–1890*, vol. 5 (Glendale, CA: Arthur H. Clark, 1986), 27.

3. Xenia Cord, "Signature Quilts," August 30, 2001, Celia Eddy's QuiltStory: Quilt-making Yesterday Today & Tomorrow, http://www.quilt.co.uk/quilting-articles.asp?idNo=20 (March 3, 2007).

Mamie Calkins

Rosie Rutledge

Mr & Mrs J. E. Conway

Bessie Adams   Teresa Weimer

Orrin Briggs

Janetta Getty

Bessie Roberts

Hulda Briggs

Grace Roberts

Hulda Calkins

Commentaries

SANDI FOX

I T WAS THE WRITTEN WORD and printed and painted images—often romanticized—that formed America's populist conception of the opening of the frontier. In addition to capturing the adventure of life and events on the overland trails, numerous diaries and journals recalled the days of departure, set down briefly and contemporaneously. When the journey was over—and sometimes decades later—accounts were occasionally drawn from those trail writings and from still vivid memories.

Catherine Scott Coburn (Kate) was thirteen years old when her family crossed the Illinois River to travel to Oregon in 1852. She published her recollections of "that trying morning of last good-byes" in the *Morning Oregonian*, June 17, 1890: "Memory returning to that morning in the long ago, paints a picture of moving wagons, of whips flourished with many a resounding snap, of men walking beside them with a forced show of indifference . . . of silently weeping women and sobbing children, and of an aged grandfather standing at his gate as the wagons filed past . . .'[1]

In his poignant genre painting *Leaving the Old Homestead*, James F. Wilkins captures an equally sentimental and detailed moment (fig. 1).[2] The dress of the two generations reveals this to be a solidly middle-class family. The father and grandfather wear buff-colored vests, in the fashion of the period, and well-fitted coats; tailoring is what set the classes apart.

The husband's averted eyes may suggest that "show of indifference." His rifle is at rest on his right shoulder, in contrast to the small, linen-lined basket he carries in his left hand, perhaps a light lunch with which to begin the journey. His wife more appropriately would be in charge of the dainty container, but she is distraught, holding her mother's hand and weeping into her handkerchief.

Circles with Points and Multiple Signatures, about 1905 (detail). See p. 105.

She hardly seems dressed for the trail. Her sunbonnet would be indispensable, of course (but with a longer "curtain" in the back to protect her neck from the wind and sun); for a journey where plain, sturdy, wool dresses without hoops or petticoats were encouraged, her dress appears much too fine. Several diaries, however, confirm that young women often chose fashionable dress (occasionally a part of their trousseau) over more practical clothing.

In Wilkins's painting, the husband, looking into the distance, is thinking perhaps of all he will gain at the end of this great adventure, his wife of all she will lose: sheer curtains behind paned, Gothic windows; a trellis heavy with green vines; and, above all, those dear faces she probably will never see again. Losses have, for her, already begun: two of her chairs have been loaded onto the wagon; the third does not fit and has been tipped over to be left behind. It is perhaps only the first of her possessions that may eventually be abandoned beside the trail.

Between wife and wagon, Wilkins has painted a small trunk; it will be the last item to be loaded and will hold those things most precious to her, either aesthetically or emotionally, one or more of which might well be her most treasured quilt. It was in such plain wooden boxes that so much of America's quilted history was carried west. These were the quilts that traveled safe and separate from the large quantity of more common bedcovers carried in the wagon to keep a westering family warm on the cold prairie nights.

Going West looks at the quilts that found their way to or were made in Nebraska in the nineteenth and early twentieth centuries. From jumping-off places such as Omaha and along the Missouri River, settlers headed to the frontier with wagon loads of items and gear that would ensure their survival. Guidebooks of the period, created specifically for overland travelers, offered lists of recommended provisions for the long journey, describing everything from foodstuffs and cooking gear to clothing and tools. One of the more formidable items to be packed were the five hundred pounds of bedding and clothing almost all of the guides suggested. Assembling such a quantity for travel, a daunting activity in itself, was a task usually shared by family and friends.

While the vast majority of surviving quilts found in Nebraska were made on this continent, several made an earlier journey across the Atlantic, with European immigrants seeking a new life. Although we can see fabrics and needlework traditions from the Old World in many quilts made in the new, it is worth our while to include a few examples of quilts made in Europe that made multiple journeys—by ship, by train, and by wagon to their final destination on the frontier.

Quilts reveal how skilled these immigrant and pioneer women were with needle and thread, but these skills were also needed to clothe themselves and their families. Women's hands were rarely idle; if a woman was sitting, her work basket was probably at her side, and her hands were stitching and knitting. A dress included in the exhibition offers a different manifestation of this skill even as its rarity reminds us that cloth from any source was likely to be recycled into quilts when the original piece became worn. A collection of doll's quilts, several made by young girls, is evidence that sewing was as much a part of a girl's education as her ABCs, and perhaps more vital to her family's comfort.

By the twentieth century, quilts would be referred to as objects of material culture, but to nineteenth-century overlanders they were as objects of sentiment rather than scholarship. The quilts on the pages that follow bear witness to such sentiment, crafted as they were for a beloved child, or the well-being of the family or by a community for the benefit a departing neighbor. They reveal the ingenuity, creativity, and above all the courage of those who made the journey west. ✷

1. Kenneth L. Holmes, ed., *Covered Wagon Women: Diaries & Letters from the Western Trails, 1840–1890*, vol. 5 (Glendale, CA: Arthur H. Clark, 1986), 28.

2. James Wilkins's extraordinary field sketches establish him as one of the greatest of the Overland Trail artists. He turned to painting saloon murals to fund his passage back East, eventually purchasing a farm in Fayette County, Illinois, where he died in his eightieth year. In his farmhouse were found his artist's oils, a picture of his farm home and "a genre piece showing a young couple and their little children leaving the old folks and the old homestead . . ." See John Francis McDermott, ed., *An Artist on the Overland Trail: The 1849 Diary and Sketches of James F. Wilkins* (San Marino, CA: Huntington Library, 1968), 19.

The Swedish Red Silk Quilt

UNIDENTIFIED MAKER
Sweden, possibly Upsula, first half 19th century
silk; quilted
80½ x 76½ (204.5 x 194.3)
Stuhr Museum of the Prairie Pioneer, Grand Island

Fig. 1 *The Swedish Red Silk Quilt* (detail)

In 1861, Swedish emigrants Charles Shieldstrom and his wife, Christine Netzel, boarded a sailing vessel for North America with the first seven of their ten children and this fine, red silk quilt. They were from a wealthy, well-educated family from whom they were distanced and disinherited when they left Sweden. Christine's maternal aunt Florin accompanied the family, and it was her small income that would provide them with the necessities of life.

A civil war was being waged in the United States, and Charles was a confirmed pacifist, so after their six-week voyage the family settled in Canada, where their last three children were born. The Shieldstroms, Aunt Florin, and the red silk quilt eventually moved from Gaspé Bay to Norwich to Presque Isle, Maine. From there they set out for Puget Sound, Washington, only to find themselves stranded, in 1877, in Merrick County, Nebraska (largely settled by disappointed gold seekers returning from California or Pike's Peak). For the next quarter-century they lived in Central

City, originally named Lone Tree for the large solitary cottonwood that stood on the banks of the Platte River.

As did so many other Swedish immigrants who arrived in Nebraska (many by a less circuitous route), they eventually bought some railroad land, this in the city of Palmer; they built a home there, their journey ended.[1] Throughout, the splendid whole-cloth quilt they carefully carried with them would have evoked memories of the comfortable life they had forfeited those many years ago. Its maker remains unknown, and indeed we do not know if the quilt belonged to Christine or to Florin. The quilt is one of great sophistication, with three strips of red silk forming its top.

Tiny, even quilting stitches sculpt an intricate and imaginative central field of interwoven, double cordlike elements. On the borders, long and rather languid leaves alternate with simple, eight-petaled flowers sparsely meandering over a stipple-quilted ground (fig. 1). This is the work of an exceptional quiltmaker, working in an atmosphere of patience and privilege.

1. Biographical information on the Shieldstrom family was presented to the Stuhr Museum by Rex Wagner, a grandson.

The Silk Mosaic Child's Quilt

ANN SARAH HARVEY BENTLEY
London, England, about 1843
silk; pieced
50½ x 42 (128.3 x 106.7)
Stuhr Museum of the Prairie Pioneer, Grand Island

Ann Sarah Harvey was the daughter of an English merchantman; he died when she was young, but her comfortable life continued when she married Peter Johnson Bentley, the son of an old Yorkshire family. They wed in 1841 when she was twenty-five years of age. The eldest of her four children, Charles Frederick Bentley, was born July 4, 1843, and it was for him she worked this lovely bit of fancy.

Construction and cloth are often significant clues as to the social status of a quiltmaker. By the end of the eighteenth century, affluent Englishwomen were enthusiastically using their leisure time to fold bits of expensive silks and chintz around hexagonal paper patterns. (The patterns were removed before the quilt was backed, but where the work was left unfinished we can determine the source of the paper that was used. In the early pieces, it was most often a combination of personal correspondence, old business ledgers and bills, and pages removed from books.) With the fabric basted over the edges of the paper grounds, the units were arranged either in a formal pattern or, as here, at random.

The fabric Ann Sarah selected was varied: floral prints, stripes, and plaids, and in both the central field and the top border a silk fondu print with yellow moving into blue.[1] The primary source of the fabric scraps was surely the prominent wholesale dry-goods firm of Robert Bentley & Co. in Cheapside, London.[2] Peter had become a member of his uncle's firm, and he had prospered.

In 1851, although in ill health, Peter and his family set out on one of the great sailing vessels bound for America. They journeyed first to Lafayette, Wisconsin, and then to Freeport, Illinois, where he bought a home and where Ann Sarah died in childbirth five years later.

For Charles Bentley and his childhood quilt, the journey was not yet over. In 1880 he and his wife, Angeline Alice, determined to settle on the Platte River. Twenty-three years earlier there was no white man within the boundaries of what would become Hall County, Nebraska, but in 1857 a group of thirty-seven pioneers arrived to establish a colony that would become the town of Grand Island. Within two years Charles and a group of influential citizens established the First National Bank of Grand Island.[3]

The child's quilt her grandmother had made a continent away descended through Charles's only daughter, Grace Bentley Paine.

1. *Ombré* (also called fondu or rainbow prints) are easily identifiable as one color shades and blends into another. Extremely popular from 1840 to 1850, quiltmakers are quick to recognize it particularly in Baltimore Album quilts. Illustrated in Susan Meller and Joost Elffers, *Textile Designs: Two Hundred Years of European and American Patterns for Printed Fabrics Organized by Motif, Style, Color, Layout, and Period* (New York: Harry N. Abrams, 1991), 96.
2. Several small, almost illegible numbers appear on the yellow/blue fondu print and elsewhere. These would seem to be salesman's samples marks.
3. Biographical information on the Bentley family is drawn primarily from A. F. Buechler and R. J. Barr, eds., *History of Hall County, Nebraska* (Lincoln, NE: Western Publishing and Engraving Co., 1920).

Maternity Dress

UNIDENTIFIED MAKER
provenance unknown, about 1840
wool and cotton
52 ¾ x 58 ⅜ (134 x 148.3)
Nebraska State Historical Society, Lincoln

For those traveling west by wagon, the time of their departure was determined not by convenience or whim or impending childbirth, but by the season during which the grasses had grown to feed the oxen along the way.[1] This meant that overland travel could safely begin only in late April or early May.

Although many women were pregnant when their great journey began, mention of those pregnancies is conspicuously scarce in their travel diaries, and the birth of a child on the trail usually is noted with only a cursory mention. Near the end of her overland journey to Washington Territory in 1853, Amelia Knight wrote, "Turn our stock out to tolerably good feed. A few days later my eighth child was born. After this we picked up and ferried across the Columbia River, utilizing a skiff, canoes and flatboat . . . This is the journey's end."[2]

There exist only a very few objects of clothing worn on the trail; most were quite simply worn out in the wearing. This brown plaid wool challis dress is a splen-

Fig. 1 *Maternity Dress*, fan pleating, center back (detail)

did exception. Significantly, details of the garment's carefully hand-sewn construction reveal it to be a maternity dress, later altered for regular wear.[3]

The bodice's detailed lining is of white cotton, adding warmth and strength; the closures originally were hooks and eyes, but now only the threads that held them remain. The original buttons, not surprisingly, have been replaced. Fan pleating at the center back (fig. 1) helped shape the bodice, and the unlined skirt is made of cartridge pleats. The set-in, shaped sleeves are lined with brown cotton and the waistband is sewn around the back and the sides, and both are trimmed with piping. It is a dressmaker's delight.

1. Those who felt the trip to the Pacific must be made in great haste, before the gold was gone and the opportunities all taken, could not wait for the grass, and sailed around the horn or crossed the Isthmus of Panama.
2. Ft. Vancouver (WA) Historical Society, *Clark County History* VI (1965):55, in Kenneth L. Holmes, ed., *Covered Wagon Women: Diaries & Letters from the Western Trails, 1840–1890*, vol. 1 (Glendale, CA: Arthur H. Clark, 1983), 12.
3. Kevin Jones of the Fashion Institute of Design & Merchandising / FIDM, Los Angeles, and Sharon Shore of Caring for Textiles, Los Angeles, joined me in a thorough inspection of the garment to confirm my initial suspicion that this was indeed a maternity dress. I thank them both.

Fringed Exaggerated Nine-Patch Quilt

UNIDENTIFIED MAKER
provenance unknown, about 1830; cotton; pieced and quilted
100 x 87¼ (256.4 x 221.6), including 3½-in. fringe
Hastings Museum of Natural and Cultural History

Blazing Star Quilt & Blazing Star Comforter

Quilt UNIDENTIFIED MAKER
provenance unknown, marked 1855
cotton; pieced and quilted
88 x 87 (223.5 x 221)
Stuhr Museum of the Prairie Pioneer,
Grand Island

Comforter UNIDENTIFIED MAKER
provenance unknown, fourth quarter
19th century; cotton and wool
pieced, tied, and embroidered
73 x 72 (185.4 x 182.9)
Hastings Museum of Natural and Cultural
History

Bedding is mentioned often in travel diaries and journals (particularly when it has been thoroughly soaked during one of the frequent prairie storms) and almost always in generic terms. A delightful and descriptive exception appears in Charlotte Pengra's diary entry of May 18, 1853. Camped "on the bank of Shell Creek," she has done a large washing, cooked two meals, and "made a pair of calico cases for pillows . . . those who come this journey should have their pillows covered with dark calico, and sheets colored, white is not suitable."[1]

In its detail, Charlotte's mention of her calico pillowcases is quite rare. In contrast to bedding, blankets, quilts, and comforters are seldom called out specifically, the references so casual that one cannot be sure the correct terminology is being applied to each object.

Blankets were easily identifiable, woven in plain or twill weave, and army blankets were among them, particularly with the influx of veterans going west following the Civil War. A young teacher in Pennsylvania,

Fig. 1 *Blazing Star Quilt* (detail)

at twenty-one Abbie Bright had a strong wish to see the American West; her brother Philip (seriously wounded during the war) urged her to join him to file her own land claim in Kansas, next to his. She traveled alone from Pennsylvania, in increments, visiting family members along the way.

Philip, she noted, had written her "only to take heavy strong clothing, and what ever I will want for a bed . . . Now my trunk is packed, It would not hold all—so a pillow with an army blanket was roaped on top."[2] Although that blanket may have belonged to Philip (or to Hiram, another brother who served), after the Civil War, blankets, like army horses (both often in worn-out condition), were no longer needed and as such were made available for public purchase; settlers frequently turned them into shirts, undershirts, and occasionally trousers.[3]

Quilts and comforters, both sewn rather than woven, seem often (and perhaps understandably) to have been misidentified one from the other. They do share certain commonalities: a multiplicity of fabrics (unless they were made of whole cloth), soft seams, and a classic repertoire of patterns—as in these two *Blazing Stars*, each surely evoking memories of the great celestial bodies that guided the overlanders across the continent. It is by the manner in which the three layers of each textile were joined that they are identified.

The carefully pieced top of the *Blazing Star Quilt* is the work of an experienced hand; the pattern itself is a technical challenge. The small red sawteeth on the border number 193, obviously an ambitious addition. The thin, pliable cotton fabric allows for the sewing together of these small diamonds and triangles, and the thin batting—usually cotton, but occasionally cotton flannel or very thin wool—permits for the fine manipulation of the needle that produced the amount and ingenuity of the multiple-patterned quilting. Fine, tiny running stitches distinguish its surface (fig. 1).

When a bedcover's top was worked in wool and/or heavy cotton, that choice of fabric generally precluded small pieces and fine quilting. With thick wool usually selected for batting, the bedcover was assembled and "tied" together with yarn or heavy string. As opposed to the delicacy of the *Blazing Star Quilt*, there is a certain

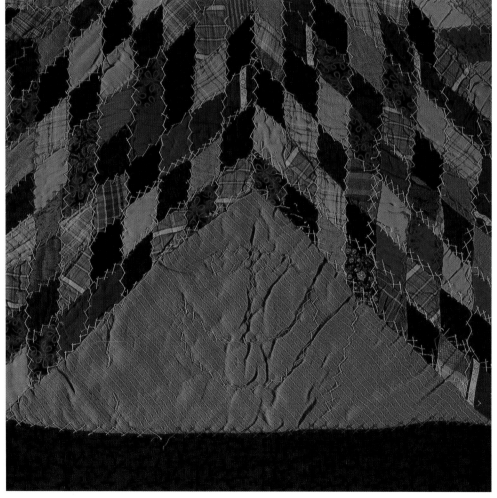

Fig. 2 *Blazing Star Comforter* (detail)

utilitarian comfort to the heavy *Blazing Star Comforter*—and indeed that is what it became, a "comforter" (or, in some regions, a "comfortable"). In its completion, its "tying" rather than "quilting" would have required much less time; this, however, seems not to have been a primary concern of its maker. She (or he) embroidered large, herringbone stitches over most seam lines and added a number of enigmatic motifs in the unpieced areas; it was these stitches that held front to back (fig. 2).

Certainly quiltmakers would have recognized the difference between quilts and comforters, but they were not always the diarists or the ones responsible for the assemblage of those five hundred pounds of bedding and clothes. Recording his 1866 journey, Charles Denney recalled washing himself in the river and then washing his clothing and his "knotted [tied?] quilt"[4]—technically a contradiction in terms. But even when the entries are nonspecific, or are in error, we are grateful that the phrases in these irreplaceable diaries and journals confirm the presence,

if not the number, of quilts and comforters on the trail:

I have spent the day writing home, tonight I'm setting with a bed quilt around my chest, hat on my head playing dice with Fred. Such is western life. Wouldn't the Whitewater falks stare in aghast?[5]

1. Charlotte Pengra, *The Diary of Charlotte Emily Stearns Pengra 1853* (Eugene, OR: Lane County Historical Society, n.d.), 20.
2. Joseph W. Snell, ed., "Roughing It on Her Kansas Claim: The Diary of Abbie Bright, 1870–1871," *Kansas Historical Quarterly* XXXVII, no. 3 (Autumn 1971): 250.
3. Everett Dick, *The Sod-House Frontier 1854–1890* (Lincoln, NE: Johnsen, 1954), 269.
4. Charles Denney, *Reminiscences and Diary*, 1875 Jan.–1883 Apr. 14–25. In 1866, Denney traveled with the John D. Holladay Company of the Church of Jesus Christ of Latter-day Saints. The company left Nebraska in mid-July and arrived in Salt Lake Valley two months later. Denney's *Reminiscences* is now in the Church Archives, Salt Lake City, Utah.
5. Ada Colvin's diary, in Kenneth L. Holmes, ed., *Covered Wagon Women: Diaries & Letters from the Western Trails, 1840–1890*, vol. 11 (Spokane, WA: Arthur H. Clark, 1993), 51.

Melissia Snyder's Floral Quilt

MELISSIA S. SNYDER
provenance unknown, 1856
cotton; appliquéd, pieced, embroidered, padded, and quilted
92 ½ x 80 ½ (235 x 204.5)
Stuhr Museum of the Prairie Pioneer, Grand Island

Fig. 1 *Melissia Snyder's Floral Quilt* (detail)

The pioneer traveler must have thought often and wistfully of the flower garden she left behind. In her prairie journal, Jean Rio Baker observed:

. . . the flowers are lifting their heads, and looking more beautiful than ever, there are a great variety of flowers growing on the prairie, such as are cultivated in our gardens at home, we are constantly walking over violets, primroses, daisy's, bluebells, the lily of the valley . . .[1]

Similarly, Amelia Hadley (on a 130-day honeymoon journey from Illinois to Oregon begun four days after her wedding) wrote, "We see almost all kinds of plants and roots that grow in our garden and green houses . . ."[2]

Quilted gardens crossed the prairie, faded flowers now. Creative in her design and construction, Melissia Snyder carefully tended to the appliquéd floral images on this mid-nineteenth-century quilt. The twelve small two-handled flowerpots that hold sparse bouquets of layered flowers have been modestly embellished with wool-embroidered chain stitches. Greater attention was paid to the flowers themselves, the edges of their overlapping petals worked in white thread in fine but-

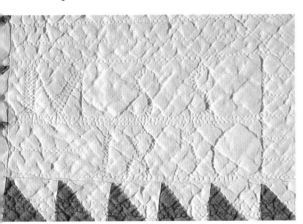

Fig. 2 *Melissia Snyder's Floral Quilt* (detail)

tonhole stitches (fig. 1). The flowerpots, segments of the flowers, and most of the leaves are padded. The central field is ambitiously framed with a sawtooth border. Eight-inch-wide strips of running vines with buds and leaves border the quilt on three sides. The work is very finely quilted, with the patterns imaginatively designed and placed, and to confirm her authorship of this ambitious piece, Melissia inscribed her initials and the date in one corner of the central field: "M.S.S. /1856" (fig. 2).

1. Kenneth L. Holmes, ed., "The Diary of Jean Rio Baker," *Covered Wagon Women: Diaries & Letters from the Western Trails, 1840–1890*, vol. 3 (Glendale, CA: Arthur H. Clark, 1984), 248.
2. Ibid., "The Journal of Amelia Hadley," 74.

Savilla Fox's Pomegranate Quilt

SAVILLA M. FOX
provenance unknown, 1866
cotton; appliquéd and quilted
88½ x 86 (224.8 x 218.4)
Fort Sidney Museum, Sidney

Savilla Fox's Pomegranate Quilt (detail)

The flora and fauna of the American West captivated explorer and settler alike. Meriwether Lewis, William Clark, and their Corps of Discovery explored the uncharted territories west of St. Louis in 1804, hoping to find passage to the Pacific Ocean. As the exhibition's cartographer, Clark mapped while Lewis meandered, botanizing and collecting specimens of extraordinary variety. Between August 17 and September 5 that year, they followed the Missouri River as it curved past the Platte toward the northwest; among the plants Lewis collected and tagged, in what would become the Nebraska counties of Burt, Dakota, Dixon, Cedar, and Knox, were the meadow anemone, the curly-top gumweed, and the large-flowered clammyweed, the wild four-o'clock and the silvery buffaloberry, the purple prairie clover and the wood's rose.[1]

Four decades later, less formally but with similar purpose and passion, a substantial number of pioneer women botanized across the country, their diaries, journals, and letters rich with their observations. Passing Fort Laramie on July 6,

1853, as she traveled from Wisconsin to Oregon, Clarissa E. Taylor posted a letter to her friend Mrs. Hadley[2]:

I wish I could paint for you a picture that would not fade of the river, the bluffs, the flats and (by far the best part) the flowers—the most beautiful and splendid, the grandest specimens of the floral kingdom.—The cactus grows here in the greatest luxuriance, and many varieties. I wish I could send you a root of the pineapple cactus. I would attempt sending more of the dried flowers, but fear they will break to pieces so you cannot distinguish them.[3]

And should Clarissa have looked in the precious trunks that carried the treasures of her fellow travelers (and perhaps in her own as well), she would have found additional "beautiful and splendid . . . specimens of the floral kingdom," these on cleverly designed and carefully appliquéd quilts.

On her vibrant quilt, Savilla Fox chose to stitch a series of stylized pomegranates, the clusters of curving sprays arranged geometrically within simple, undulating borders. In small stitches of white thread, she quilted her name (Savilla M. Fox), the date (1866), and, tucked between petals and leaves, a sentimental series of tiny hearts.

1. Gary E. Moulton, ed., *Herbarium of the Lewis & Clark Expedition*, vol. 12, *The Journals of the Lewis & Clark Expedition* (Lincoln and London: University of Nebraska Press, 1999), 314; Thomas Schmidt and Jeremy Schmidt, *The Saga of Lewis & Clark: Into the Uncharted West* (New York: D. K. Publishing, 1999), 208.
2. From the fort, letters could be sent back to friends left behind, and Mrs. Hadley made sure Clarissa's was shared with others by having it published in the *Watertown Chronicle* the following month.
3. S. H. Taylor, "Oregon Bound," *Oregon Historical Quarterly* (1921): 136–38.

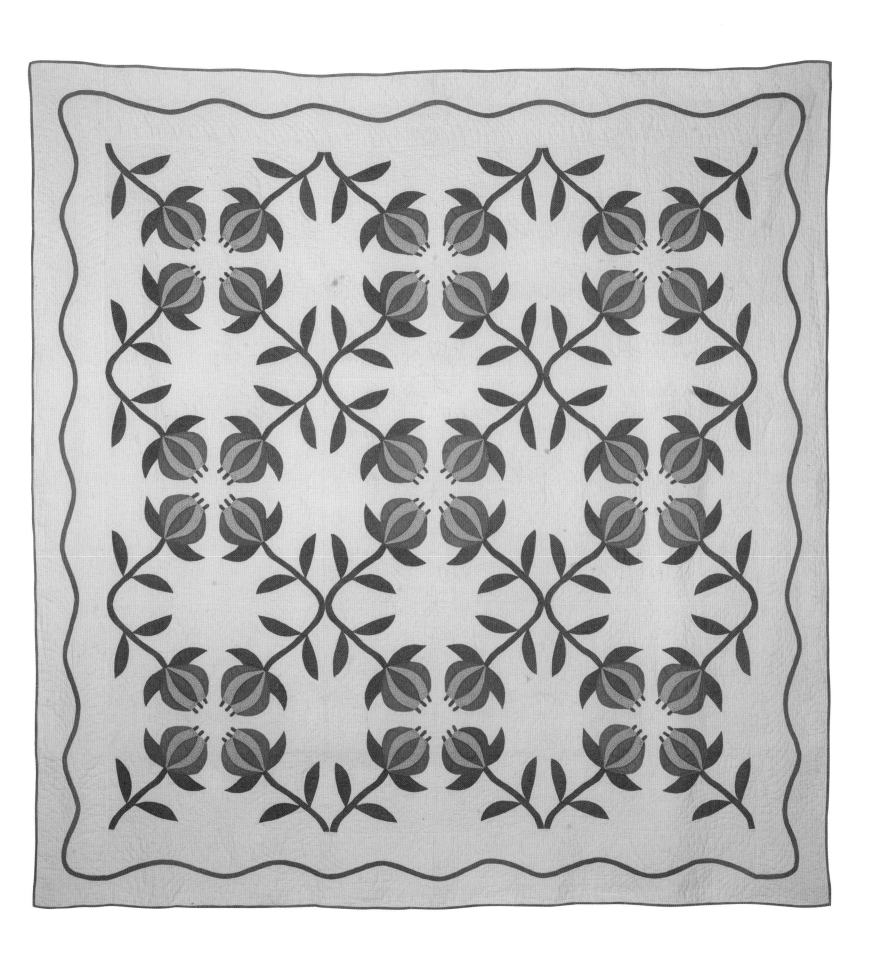

The "Prince's Feathers" Quilt

MADE BY OR FOR SARAH MCMANUS BILLINGER
probably Preble County, Ohio, mid-19th century
cotton; appliquéd and quilted
87 x 89 (221 x 226.1)
Gage County Historical Society Museum, Beatrice

Meriwether Lewis, of the famed Lewis and Clark Expedition, would have been pleased to see the huge, stylized prince's-feathers appliquéd in the middle of the nineteenth century by (or for) Sarah McManus Billinger; large, showy flowers were his particular favorites. Indeed, the quilt was worked in an Ohio county whose early histories made note of the ground "jeweled with strange and brilliant flowers" beneath the giant oaks and the sycamores, walnuts, and chestnuts.[1]

In the spring of 1823, John C. McManus, Esq., settled with Catherine, his wife of eight years, in the wilderness of Jackson Township, Preble County, Ohio. On heavily forested land with no roads and few neighbors, they built a successful farm on which they would spend the rest of their lives. John labored as a surveyor, a justice of the peace, an attorney traveling the county circuit by horseback, and a farmer. When he died in 1852 at age sixty-five, he was buried in the old Frame graveyard, eventually joined by the other first-settlers of the township.[2]

As was typical of those early years, much less is known about Catherine Miley McManus. Her family had migrated to Ohio from Pennsylvania, traveling down the Ohio River on a keelboat; she married John C. McManus in 1815; she was a Methodist; she survived many years beyond her husband, becoming one of the oldest living pioneers in the township; and she was the mother of eleven children. Sarah Ann was her oldest daughter and it was by, or for, her that this quilt was made.

Sarah, born in 1819, became a young widow when her first husband, Daniel Brower, was accidentally killed about six months after their marriage. In 1841 she married William Billinger, and in 1857, traveling in a covered wagon, they moved onto the unsettled Illinois prairie, eventually establishing a prosperous farm in Woodford County.[3]

Unless a quilt is discreetly signed, authorship after a century and a half is often impossible to confirm, and this is the case with the "Prince's Feathers." The quilt is attributed to Sarah McManus Billinger, but it also could have been given to Sarah as the work of a loving mother. Eight of Sarah's ten children survived, and by 1889 two had gone west: Frank and his wife to farm, and her daughter Sarah to teach, both in Phelps County, Nebraska. The quilt probably moved west with one or the other.

1. Albert Adams Graham, *History of Preble County, Ohio* (Cleveland: H. Z. Williams & Bro., Publishers, 1881), 27.
2. Ibid., 68–69, 252. The graveyard developed around the small grave of the infant daughter of John and Polly Frame who died in 1816; with no cemetery in the neighborhood, John dug a little grave in a secluded spot near their house, soon to become overgrown with heavy brush.
3. *Portrait and Biographical Album of Woodford County, Illinois* (Chicago: Chapman Bros., 1889), 218–19.

The Civil War Quilt

UNIDENTIFIED MAKER
provenance unknown, about 1860
cotton; appliquéd and quilted
85 x 85 (215.9 x 215.9)
Gage County Historical Society Museum, Beatrice

Joseph Miller had moved from Pennsylvania to Noble County, Ohio, as a boy of fourteen. On November 29, 1861, he joined the Union army and enlisted in the newly organized 78th Ohio Volunteer Infantry, and when Co. G marched off to join General Sherman's army, Joseph, age nineteen, marched with it.[1]

At some point in the midst of that long and dreadful war, Joseph was given one of the great treasures of his young life. On one bitterly cold evening, the men were sent out to surrounding farm homes to ask for blankets. To Joseph came this splendid appliquéd quilt. A stylized floral pattern is repeated on each of the sixteen large (17½-inch) blocks. The curving pieces of red, yellow, and green cottons were affixed to the white ground with tiny running stitches on the turned edges. Finely quilted over both pattern and ground, the parallel lines are a scant one quarter inch apart—the result of a quiltmaker's best effort. Perhaps the farmwife was overcome with the patriotic fervor sweeping the country; perhaps it is what she hoped would be

given to a son of her own should he find himself knocking on a stranger's door. Its bright colors were almost obliterated by the filth of the battlefields, but its fabric remained whole. After the war, soaked and scrubbed, the quilt was carried by the young man throughout the next half-century of his life.

Joseph had been promoted from private to corporal to sergeant and then to orderly sergeant, and finally to first lieutenant in command of Co. F. Following the surrender of Confederate general Joe Johnston's army, the 78th regiment moved through Richmond to Washington, D.C., where they participated in the Grand Review on May 24, 1865. One hundred fifty thousand soldiers from General George Meade's Army of the Potomac and General William Tecumseh Sherman's Army of Georgia and Army of the Tennessee marched among the flags in the Union victory parade—and Joseph Miller marched with them.

Mustered out of the army on July 16, 1865, in Columbus, Ohio, Joseph and his quilt began moving west: in August of that

year to Owen County, Indiana, where he formally committed to the Methodist church and where, on March 17, 1867, he married Miss Martha Elmira Scott; in 1870 to Maryville in Andrew County, Missouri; in 1872 to homesteading in Polk County, Nebraska; and in October 1898 to Beatrice, Nebraska, where he died, noted the *Daily Express*, "an old soldier" on September 24, 1913, at the age of seventy-one years, one month, and twenty-six days. His widow, his daughter Angie, and his quilt survived him.[2]

1. Miller wrote a four-page letter, dated June 23, 1864, describing his experiences on march with the 78th Ohio. That letter (MS 89-076) is now in the Digital Library and Archives, University Libraries, Virginia Polytechnic Institute and State University. It was in an envelope addressed to "Rev Wright / Batesville / Noble Co Ohio" and postmarked "Louisville, KY. Jul [8?] 1864."

2. Information on Mr. Miller's military promotions and his travels following the war was gathered from a number of obituaries following his death, and that of his wife in 1924.

Nine-Patch Blocks with Sawtooth Border

ANNA L. SMITH
Northwestern New York, about 1869
cotton; pieced
12¼ x 8⅝ (31.1 x 21.9)
Loup County Historical Society, Taylor

In March 1884, immigrants were moving into the Sandhills area of north-central Nebraska. Following a sandy trail beside the North Loup River, two heavy wagons carried the earthly possessions and the family of Edwin B. Smith into Blaine County. Edwin set about to plow and to plant; his wife, Anna, to make a home in a one-room pine-board shack.

With modest prosperity seemingly within their grasp, a springtime wind brought the scent of burning grass to the Smiths and their scattered neighbors. Prairie fire! The flames stopped only when they had reached the riverbanks. Despite buckets and tubs of water, the fire engulfed the barn, shed, outbuildings, and lumber, along with a wagon of ear corn. Frantic, Edwin's fine team of horses had galloped into the smoke and flames, and the cattle had dispersed or died.

Miraculously, the house itself emerged intact, saving one of Anna's girlhood treasures: this small, pieced doll quilt, which she had made when she was nine years old. It was where she had begun to learn her skills as a quiltmaker: simple nine-patches were set and sashed and encased within a classic sawtooth border.

Nebraska pioneers were of sturdy stuff and most were somehow able to survive prairie fires and grasshoppers, blizzards and tornadoes, hailstorms and rising rivers. Anna and Edwin survived, and they prospered. Edwin developed one of Blaine County's largest cattle ranches; Anna cultivated for herself a wide range of domestic pleasures and pastimes. She planted flower gardens and embroidered, knit sweaters and socks for "the boys" in World War I, and continued to quilt. For almost a century, a number of ladies from Blaine and Loup counties attended meetings of the Clever Clique Club, gathering in each others' homes. For pioneer women, particularly in such sparsely populated counties, such organizations were socially and creatively significant, and Anna was one of the club's earliest members.[1]

Although organized as a "sewing" club, quilting was in particular favor at the Clever Clique Club. One member avowed,

"I'd as soon not go to club if I can't quilt." Traveling throughout the counties to the monthly meetings in a horse and buggy was a lengthy challenge. "Crowds of 50 to 60 women, men and children were not unusual because club days included a huge potluck dinner and plenty of visiting time for the gents."[2]

Anna lived in Blaine County for fifty years. In later years she would sit with her husband on their flower-encircled porch, Edwin reading an issue of the *Nebraska Farmer*.[3]

1. Kevin Brown, "Legends & Landmarks: The Clever Clique Ladies of Loup and Blaine Counties," *The Grand Island Independent* (September 18, 2003): 14–15.
2. Ibid.
3. Staple reading material for rural farmers, the *Nebraska Farmer* was published by Samuel R. McKelvie, a Nebraska-born, two-term Republican governor. McKelvie's magazine encouraged farmers to take advantage of technological advances in agriculture and to follow good business procedures. Frederick C. Luebke, *Nebraska: An Illustrated History* (Lincoln: University of Nebraska Press, 2005), 250–51.

Nine-Patch Blocks with Sawtooth Border   57

The Double Hearts Quilt

MRS. JAMES ANDERSON
probably Grant City, Missouri, about 1874
cotton; appliquéd, pieced, and quilted; 81 x 65 ½ (205.7 x 166.4)
Hastings Museum of Natural and Cultural History

Silk Mosaic Quilt

UNIDENTIFIED MAKER
provenance unknown, fourth quarter 19th century
silk; pieced, quilted, and embroidered; 83⅜ x 71¼ (211.8 x 181)
Durham Western Heritage Museum, Omaha

Pieced Quilt, Concentric Strips and Triangles

MRS. THOMAS MERCER
about 1875; cotton; 76½ x 75 (194.3 x 190.5)
Washington County Historical Association, Fort Calhoun

"LeMoyne Star" with Embroidered Sashing

MRS. SILAS A. STRICKLAND
about 1880; silk and velvet
60¼ x 52 (153.2 x 132.1)
Durham Western Heritage Museum, Omaha

Log Cabin, "Barn Raising" Variation

UNIDENTIFIED MAKER
1882; cotton, silk, wool, velvet
74 x 65 ½ (188 x 166.4)
Stuart White Horse Museum

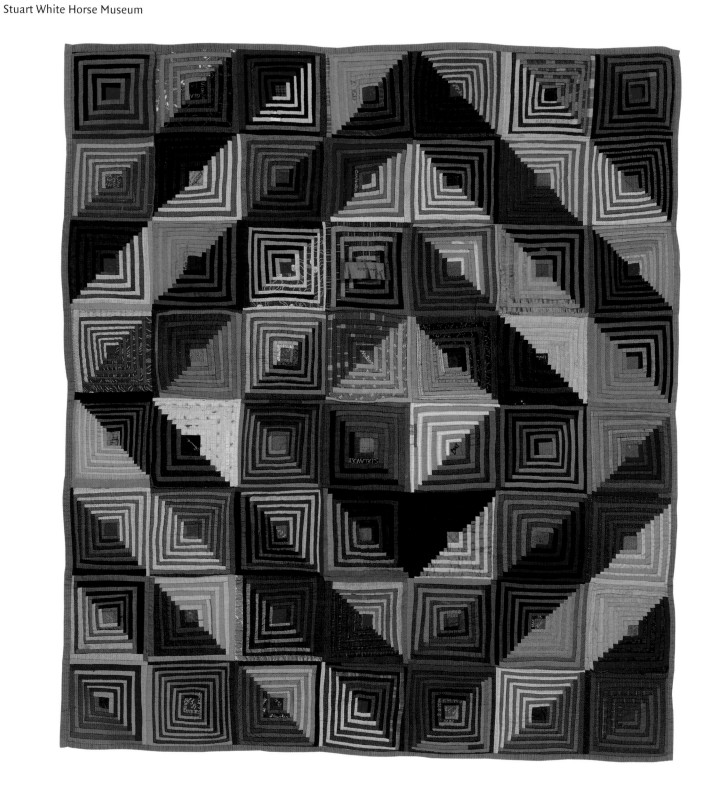

Anvil Doll Bedcover

UNIDENTIFIED MAKER
provenance unknown, late 19th century
cotton; pieced
21¾ x 17½ (55.3 x 44.5)
Historical Society of Garden County, Oshkosh

Fig. 1 Unidentified maker, *Log Cabin Child's Quilt (Pineapple Variation)*, provenance unknown, late 19th century, wool challis; pressed, pieced, and tied, 30¼ x 28¼ (76.8 x 71.8). Sarpy County Historical Museum, Bellevue

Fig. 2 Unidentified maker, *"LeMoyne Star" Child's Quilt*, provenance unknown, second half 19th century, cotton; pieced and quilted, 45½ x 38 (115.6 x 96.5). Durham Western Heritage Museum, Omaha

I remember my two older sisters and me sleeping on a splintery board floor in the northwest corner of the sod-house, and I remember crawling onto a

tick that had rustling stuff in it. We three children had a feather filled cover and I sucked and chewed on one of the corners of that quilt. The three of us fought—each one wanted to suck a particular corner. Finally we felt each other's warmth and went to sleep.[1]

Their own small quilts were of comfort to pioneer children (figs. 1, 2), as were their dolls, plain or fancy. Like their owners,

dolls often were placed in peril; the store-bought doll dropped beside the bundle at the mother's feet in James Wilkins's *Leaving the Old Homestead* (see p. 34) would have been retrieved to join the family in the wagon.

Quiltmakers have always used "bits and pieces" to construct something small with which to delight a child; the five hundred pounds of bedding assembled for the journey certainly would have allowed the inclusion of a small doll quilt.[2] Doll quilts of the nineteenth century seldom depicted childish whimsies. In pattern and palette they were, quite simply, large quilts sewn small. Worked within the female community, they were stitched by loving mothers or grandmothers, sisters or aunts—and eventually by the child herself, almost as soon as she could hold a needle (figs. 3–6).

The gentlemen, however, were not to be outdone. As a boy during the winter of 1852–53, Ira T. Paine stitched a bit of piecework (fig. 7); he gave it to his granddaughter Alice Ella Paine in 1928. To hold dolls and their tiny quilts, two indulgent fathers

Fig. 3 Unidentified maker, *Reversible Doll Quilt*, about 1890, cotton, 25 x 18 (63.5 x 45.7). North Platte Valley Museum, Gering

Fig. 4 Unidentified maker, *Mosaic Doll Quilt*, about 1910, cotton, 23 x 16½ (58.4 x 41.9). High Plains Historical Museum, McCook

Fig. 5 Unidentified maker, *"LeMoyne Star" Doll Quilt*, about 1900, cotton, 17¼ x 12 (43.9 x 30.5). Hastings Museum of Natural and Cultural History

or grandfathers, brothers or uncles utilized small, well-worn boxes that once held their wives' cinnamon (fig. 8) and their own cigars (fig. 9) to construct the dearest of cradles.

1. Lillian Schlissel et al., *Far From Home: Families of the Westward Journey* (New York: Schocken Books, 1989), 210.
2. For an extensive, illustrated discussion, see Sandi Fox, *Small Endearments: Nineteenth-century Quilts for Children and Dolls*, 2nd ed. (Nashville, TN: Rutledge Hill Press, 1994), 156–67.

Fig. 7 Ira T. Paine, *Doll Quilt Top*, provenance unknown, 1852–53, cotton; pieced, 16 x 13 (40.6 x 33). Stuhr Museum of the Prairie Pioneer, Grand Island

Fig. 6 Orpha Morgan, *"Hanging Diamonds" Doll Quilt*, about 1900, cotton, 23 x 14½ (58.4 x 36.8). Plains Historical Society, Kimball

Fig. 8 Howard Mortimore, *Cinnamon Box Doll Cradle*, Nebraska, about 1908–25, wood and nails, 7 x 7 ½ x 10 ½ (17.8 x 19.1 x 26.7). Nebraska State Historical Society, Lincoln

Fig. 9 Unidentified maker, *Cigar Box Cradle*, probably Nebraska, about 1900, wood and nails, 4 x 3 ¾ x 7 ¾ (10.2 x 9.5 x 19.7). Nebraska State Historical Society, Lincoln

Wagon Wheels Crazy Quilt

SARA BARBARY GOOD BOLDON
Craig, Burt County, Nebraska, about 1890
wool; pieced, tied, pressed, and embroidered
74 x 66 (188 x 167.6)
Burt County Museum, Tekamah

Sara and James Boldon left Indiana to farm, and to raise nine children, in Burt County, Nebraska, near the Logan River. At the end of the nineteenth century, Sara styled a wonderful wool crazy quilt. Twenty-four-and-one-half-inch circular images dominate the central field; throughout, the variety of wool worsted fabrics are cleverly embroidered in worsted wool yarns. In choosing the wagon wheel as her primary motif, she chose the iconic image of the trail that had brought them to Burt County all those years ago.

As the great, heavy-laden wagons moved out from their jumping-off places, they were filled to the brim with the practical and the necessary—the objects that would assure survival on the trail and success where the trail ended. The overlanders were guided in their selection of supplies by the hundreds of travel guides printed throughout the nineteenth century,[1] by letters sent back from earlier travelers that were published in local newspapers, and, in the case of the Mormons, by the Church of Jesus Christ of Latter-day Saints, which arranged for the migration of an entire,

and immense, religious community. In Nauvoo, Illinois, where the Mormons gathered, wagonwrights worked between August 1845 and the end of January 1846 to build two thousand wagons.[2]

For overland travelers, the wagon was, of course, the most important item to be considered, and most were patterned after that designed and constructed by the great St. Louis wagon master Joseph Murphy. It was on the Murphy wagon that the Mormon wagon was based, except for the frequent addition of a bar on the back to hold small trees and saplings.[3]

The westering wife usually had a vital task in the preparation of the wagon: constructing the waterproof cover that would be supported by five or six bent hickory bows. Another of the feminine tasks was the assembling of foodstuffs, mostly into the sacks she had sewn for that purpose, and, looming large, arranging for the five hundred pounds of clothing and bedding that almost all of the travel guides suggested—a daunting activity usually shared by family and friends. As Catherine Scott Coburn wrote in the *Morning Oregonian*, June 17, 1890:

Through all the winter preceding the April morning when the final start was made, the fingers of the women and girls were busy providing additional stores of bedding and blankets, of stockings and sunbonnets, of hickory shirts and gingham aprons . . . the heartaches that were stitched and knitted and woven into them, through the brief winter afternoons, as relatives that were to be left behind and friends of a lifetime dropped in to lend a hand in the awesome undertaking of getting ready for a journey that promised no return . . .[4]

1. See Ray A. Billington, "Books That Won the West," *The American West: Magazine of the Western History Association* IV, no. 3 (August 1967).
2. Richard E. Bennett, *We'll Find the Place: The Mormon Exodus 1846–1848* (Salt Lake City, UT: Deseret Book Co., 1997), 51. For a "Bill of Particulars for the Emigrants Leaving This Government Next Spring," see the *Nauvoo Neighbor*, October 29, 1845. The bill, an itemized list of provisions for the journey that describes everything from food items and bedding to cooking gear, clothing, and tools, conveys the sheer logistical complexity of an overland journey.
3. Bennett, *We'll Find the Place*.
4. Kenneth L. Holmes, ed., *Covered Wagon Women: Diaries & Letters from the Western Trails, 1840–1890*, vol. 5 (Glendale, CA: Arthur H. Clark, 1986), 27.

"Wagon Wheels" and "Dresden Plates" on a Crazy Quilt Ground

UNIDENTIFIED MAKER
late 19th century; wool, velvet
82 x 60 (208.3 x 152.4)
Burt County Museum, Tekamah

Pyramid of Red and White Signature Blocks

INDEPENDENT ORDER OF ODD FELLOWS (I.O.O.F.) MEMBERS
1890; cotton
74½ x 71 (189.2 x 180.3)
Fairbury City Museum

The Pawnee City Newspaper Quilt

UNIDENTIFIED MAKER
Pawnee City, Pawnee County, Nebraska, 1890–92
cotton; embroidered
81¼ x 67½ (206.4 x 171.5)
Pawnee City Historical Society and Museum

Fig. 1 *The Pawnee City Newspaper Quilt* (detail)

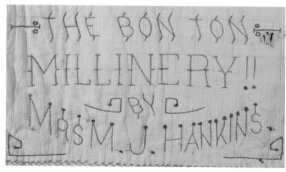
Fig. 2 *The Pawnee City Newspaper Quilt* (detail)

Fig. 3 *The Pawnee City Newspaper Quilt* (detail)

The frontier newspapers chronicled the settlement and the development of the American West. The first published in Pawnee City, Nebraska, in 1868, was the *Pawnee Tribune*; changed to the *Pawnee Republican* in 1872, it continues to publish today as the fifth oldest newspaper in the state. Its name appears on this enigmatic textile, as do those of the *Pawnee Independent* ("Published in the Interests of the Farmers and Other Laboring Classes / $1.50 Per Year") and the *Pawnee Press*, "The People's Popular Paper."[1]

The style of the "ads" on this quilt bears great similarity to the graphics of the newspaper advertisements of the period. The quilt is in all probability a fund-raiser, but although two dates appear (1890 and 1892) there is no indication of quiltmaker, sponsor, or purpose, either on the quilt itself or in extant copies of the *Pawnee Republican*.[2]

Many establishments bought textile ads to promote their business interests, including Agnew Bros., "dealers in fine footware"; the Bon Ton Millinery "by Mrs. M. J. Hankins"; and Walter C. Kern, "dealer in watches, jewelry, clocks, spectacles, silverware, gold pens" (figs. 1–3).

In addition to businesses, numerous personal and political entries are included—the Methodist Ladies Social Union (fig. 4), the 1890 Pawnee city clerks, the postmistress, the faculty and trustees of the Pawnee City Academy, the 1890 Pawnee County officials (judge, sheriff, treasurer, clerk, superintendent, attorney, and clerk of courts)—strengthening the quilt's significance as one of the city's historical documents.

If the quilt was raffled off, we do not know who won it; if it was a presentation quilt, we do not know to whom it was given. We only know that someone kept it safe for decades, and during the next century someone unidentified left it on the steps of the Pawnee City Post Office.

1. A booklet published in 1957 in honor of the Pawnee City Centennial notes that at the end of the nineteenth century the town published six newspapers: three weeklies, two dailies, and a semiweekly.
2. Carol A. Sisco, current editor of the *Pawnee Republican*, generously researched the papers from 1890 through the first quarter of 1893, but found no mention of a quilt.

Fig. 4 *The Pawnee City Newspaper Quilt* (detail)

The Omaha Commerce Quilt

LADIES AID SOCIETY OF THE GRACE EVANGELICAL LUTHERAN CHURCH
Omaha, Douglas County, Nebraska, 1895
cotton; pieced, embroidered, and quilted
94 x 81 (238.8 x 205.7)
Durham Western Heritage Museum, Omaha

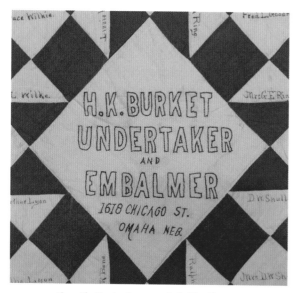

Fig. 1 *The Omaha Commerce Quilt* (detail)

In August 1859, Abraham Lincoln stood on a bluff in Iowa, looking across the Missouri River at Omaha, a small frontier town in Nebraska Territory. Traveling for business and political reasons (he was an unannounced candidate for the 1860 Republican presidential nomination), he had no wish to actually cross the river to visit the rough little town. He had seen such places all his life.[1]

Omaha was a jumping-off place to the West where wagons could be outfitted and traveling companies formed. The early settlers were more interested in developing the town's commercial opportunities than in establishing a sense of community. Two blocks on Farnam Street, the original main street, were soon lined with businesses catering to the overlanders: mercantile houses, banks, hotels, and saloons. In contrast, the pioneers lived in log cabins, sod houses, and dugouts, most of them unkempt; a man from Michigan was ridiculed when he planted ornamental shrubs on his property.[2]

Immigrants arrived in large numbers, but they moved on; community began in the West when the travelers stayed. In 1866, Omaha was more of a tranquil village: Farnam Street had its business establishments as well as a reassuring sign of settlement and community: a high-steeple church.

In a fund-raising effort, the Ladies Aid Society of the Grace Evangelical Lutheran Church in South Omaha pieced, embroi-

dered, and quilted a selective city directory. Forty-two commercial establishments appear to have purchased "advertisements" in support of the project, with many of the businesses located on Farnam Street.

The businesses on the quilt were diverse and prosperous. When W. R. Bennett and Co. was established in 1878 ("a wholesale and retail dealer in everything useful, ornamental and staple"), its two partners and one assistant were adequate to handle the business.[3] H. K. Burket, "Undertaker and Embalmer" (fig. 1), came to Omaha in 1883 and was the longest established funeral director in the city. And among the early established businesswomen, Mrs. J. Benson began in 1887 dealing in furnishings, fancy dry goods, and notions.[4]

1. Lawrence H. Larsen and Barbara J. Cottrell, *The Gate City: A History of Omaha* (Lincoln: University of Nebraska Press, 1982), 33–35.
2. Ibid., 35.
3. James W. Savage, John T. Bell, and Consul W. Butterfield, *History of the City of Omaha, Nebraska, and South Omaha* (New York, Chicago: Munsell, 1894), 469.
4. Ibid., 466, 490.

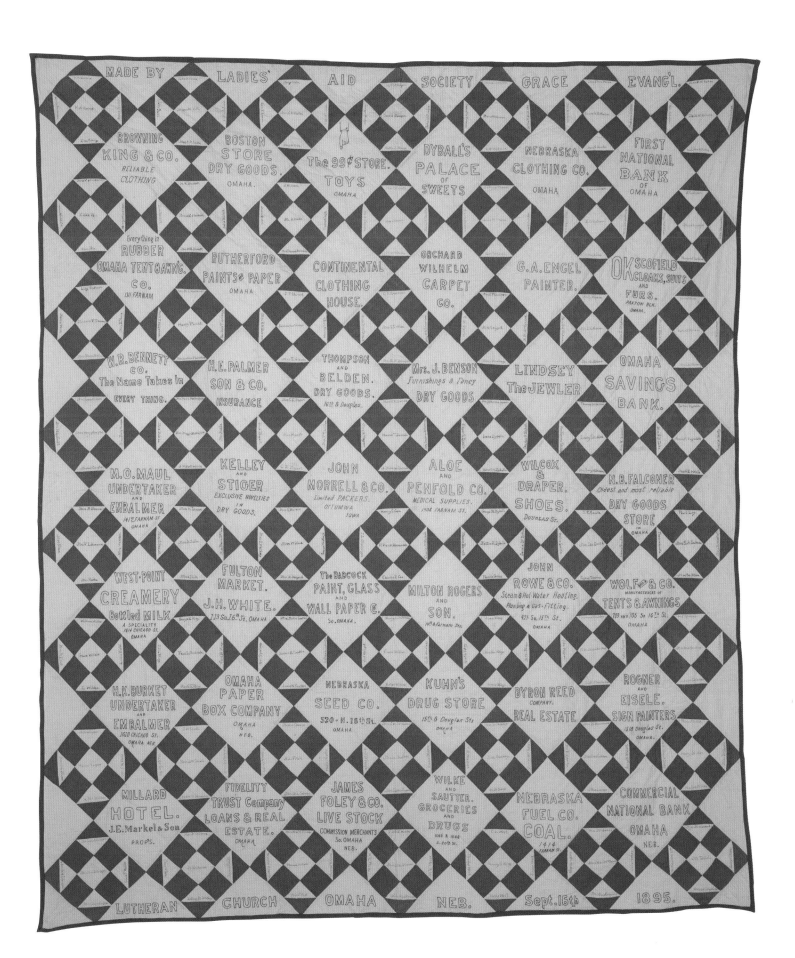

Mary Norris's "Blazing Star" Quilt

MARY MAGDALENE MOOK NORRIS
Sandusky County, Ohio, about 1895
cotton; pieced, piped, and quilted
73 x 73 (185.4 x 185.4)
Nebraska State Historical Society, Lincoln

Many families were drawn West by letters describing the good land their kinfolk had found there, and for months during the autumn and winter of 1845, Chauncey and Mary Norris discussed leaving Batavia, New York, to join her brothers in Sandusky County, Ohio. In the early summer, having lost a month-old daughter, they left with their three remaining children and a few bits of furniture to carve a farm out of the thick timber they would find in the "Black Swamp" country.

Mary held her children very dear, and 1864 would prove a tragic year for the family. Their eldest child, John Henry, fought for the Union with the 55th Ohio Volunteer Infantry. Wounded in the battle of Resaca, Georgia, he succumbed to infection, and was dead at the age of twenty-five. That same year, Mary's husband, Chauncey, died of pneumonia.[1]

Her remaining son, George, called "Willie" within his family, was only three years old when his father died, and he later wrote that after that awful year, he never heard his mother sing, or even hum a tune. George eventually moved farther west to practice law and politics, and as a Nebraska senator distinguished himself on the national scene for forty years.

We seldom find physical evidence of a pattern name assigned to an early quilt by the quiltmaker herself,[2] and we have no note or diary entry to tell us what name (if any) Mary Norris might have assigned to this splendid star quilt pieced for "Willie's" oldest daughter, Hazel. Small diamonds cut from common calico were sewn together to form eight larger diamonds, these uniquely separated by piping (fig. 1).

Regional and period preferences often determined the name of a particular quilt pattern. These great stars were among the most extravagant and sophisticated of America's earliest pieced quilts, made large and often of floral chintz fabrics. Meriwether Lewis himself had found a flower called blazing star in what would be Lyman or Brule County, South Dakota, on September 15, 1804.[3]

Early references to "blazing star" would have been logical in this period of great and seldom-understood celestial activities; an 1898 article in the *Essex Antiquarian* cites contemporary responses to the comets seen over New England in the latter part of the seventeenth century, noting how "Night after night, the whole winter through, 'the great blazing starre' took

its position in the southern sky as soon as the stars began to glint in the evening constellations."[4]

But although Mary surely would have been aware of the great swarms of comets that had streaked across the country from 1833 to 1866, it is doubtful she made this quilt in celebration of any such event. When Mary (a farmwife for much of her life) worked this sturdy cotton quilt, at the very end of the nineteenth century, she might have looked not up but down to blooming blazing stars.

1. George W. Norris, *Fighting Liberal: The Autobiography of George W. Norris* (New York: Macmillan, 1945), 10. Most of the biographical details of this quiltmaker's life are drawn from her son's autobiography.
2. Although a specific quilt pattern might be referred to by an outside observer, more often the quilt was identified on personal terms: "Mary's star quilt," for example.
3. Gary E. Moulton, ed., *Herbarium of the Lewis & Clark Expedition*, vol. 12, *The Journals of the Lewis & Clark Expedition* (Lincoln and London: University of Nebraska Press, 1999), 314. In his book *Plants of the Lewis & Clark Expedition* (Missoula, MT: Mountain Press, 2003), H. Wayne Phillips includes detailed information on three variations of blazing star collected and tagged by Lewis, including pertinent excerpts from the Lewis and Clark journals: Blazing Star, 48; Rough Blazing Star, 60, and Tall Blazing Star, 66.
4. "The Early Comets," *Essex Antiquarian* (1898), 75.

OVERLEAF: Fig. 1 *Mary Norris's "Blazing Star" Quilt* (detail)

Mary Norris's "Blazing Star" Quilt   79

The G.A.R. Flag Quilt

PROBABLY MADE BY THE WOMAN'S RELIEF CORPS
Grand Island, Hall County, Nebraska, marked 1898
cotton; pieced, appliquéd, and quilted; embroidered signatures
67¾ x 86¼ (172.1 x 219.1)
Stuhr Museum of the Prairie Pioneer, Grand Island

Drawn to Nebraska Territory by the 1862 Homesteading Act, large numbers of Civil War veterans found new communities of comrades through membership in the Grand Army of the Republic (GAR)—the largest and most influential of the groups formed by Union veterans following the war. Established originally as a social and fraternal organization, members directed their efforts toward veterans' needs and, importantly, to the enshrinement of the flag as America's principal patriotic icon.

During the war, the "cult of the flag" swept across the country. The *New Orleans Picayune* (April 17, 1861) declared the nation to be in the patriotic grip of "flagmania." Both Union and Confederate flags were sewn in abundance by the clever ladies and girls of both sides—to be hung from buildings, to be given to soldiers as they departed for the fight, and to adorn the seamstress's own person. In Baton Rouge, Louisiana, in 1862, Sarah Morgan Dawson wore a small Confederate flag "pinned to my bosom. The man who says take it off will have to pull it off for him-self; the man attempts it—well! A pistol in my pocket fills the gap!"[1]

The 1864 Fourth of July celebration in San Francisco was observed by Mark Twain, a reporter for the *San Francisco Daily Morning Call*, who described the flag-bedecked frenzy as one of "magnificence, enthusiasm, crowds, noise, wind and dust." He found the entire city "swathed in a waving drapery of flags" and Montgomery Street "no longer a street of compactly built houses, but simply a quivering cloud of gaudy red and white stripes, which shut out from view almost everything but itself. Some houses were broken out all over with flags like small-pox patients. . . . "[2]

By 1867, the GAR was organizing state and national conventions called encamp-ments, and this handsome flag quilt, worked in 1898 (most likely within the organization's female auxiliary), probably commemorated one such event. It may have been initiated as a fund-raiser (for a modest sum the contributor could have his name inscribed on the surface of the quilt) or worked as an individual memento. Because the GAR fervently hoped to have an American flag emblazoned on, or hang-ing from, every available surface, public and private, it was of course appropriate that twenty flags of "gaudy red and white stripes" formed the surface of this quilt.

1. Sarah Morgan Dawson, *A Confederate Girl's Diary* (Boston: Houghton Mifflin, 1913), 24.
2. Marc Leepson, *Flag: An American Biography* (New York: Thomas Dunne Books/St. Martin's Press, 2005), 107.

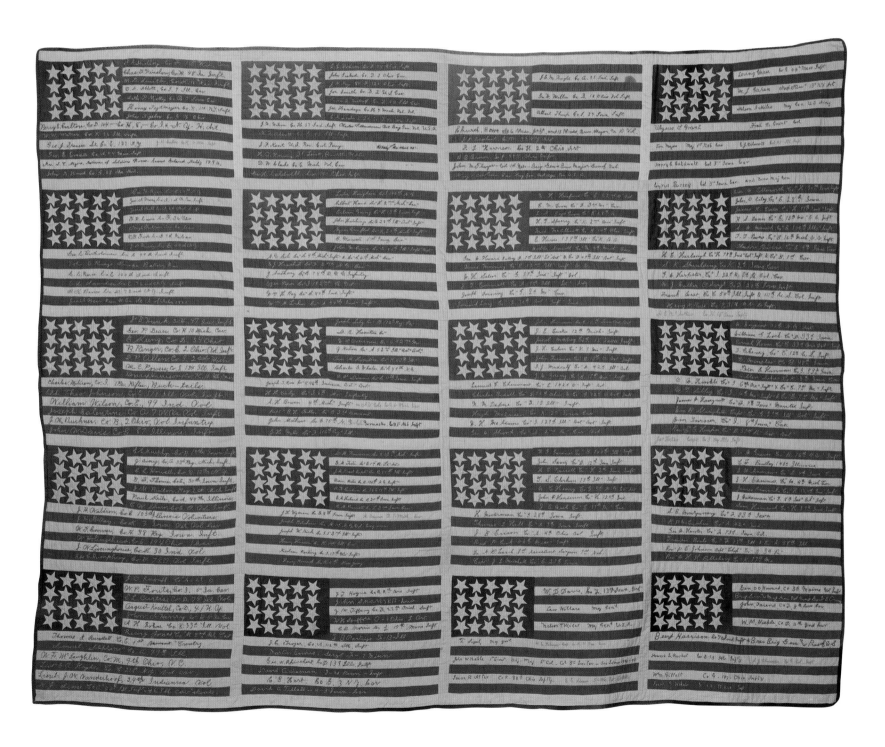

The Trans-Mississippi Exposition Quilt

LADIES AID SOCIETY OF THE METHODIST EPISCOPAL CHURCH
Valentine, Cherry County, Nebraska, 1898
cotton; primarily machine embroidered
80 x 96 (203.2 x 243.8)
Cherry County Historical Museum, Valentine

During the 1890s, the frontier farms and towns of Nebraska survived an economic depression, a drought, and the grasshoppers. Inspired to move their city beyond its frontier image, in the fall of 1895, Omaha's businessmen and politicians determined that the city would present a Trans-Mississippi and International Exposition and step, progressively, into the twentieth century.

The ambitious project, with representation from thirty-one states and several foreign countries, was realized in grand style. Beaux-Arts buildings arose on almost two hundred acres on a bluff overlooking the Missouri's floodplain. A correspondent for *Harper's Weekly*, perhaps expecting a pioneer motif, was overwhelmed by the "great buildings . . . classic in their architecture and rich in ornament," and avowed that "this is not an exposition of the common commercial type. It is something much higher, and keenly sympathetic with higher elements of life."[1] Although the buildings exuded a sense of permanence, they had in fact been artfully constructed of wood,

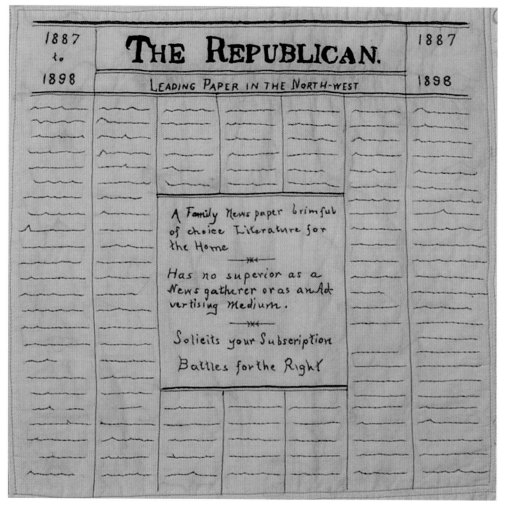

Fig. 1 *The Trans-Mississippi Exposition Quilt* (detail)

Fig. 2 *The Trans-Mississippi Exposition Quilt* (detail)

Merchandise, Geo. Schwalm Meat Market (fig. 2), J. W. Yeast Hardware and Saddles, and others.

The advertisement for A. G. Shaw Photographer (fig. 3) unexpectedly reminds us that although the exposition did not celebrate the frontier, on the other side of Nebraska in areas such as the Sandhills, aspects and images of the frontier still existed. Captain Amberson G. Shaw (1842–1925) was a cavalryman, a scout and an interpreter, a freighter and a trader, a craftsman and a carpenter. As a businessman arriving in Valentine in 1884, he established the town's first photographic gallery and advertised in the June 18, 1886, issue of *The Blade*: "Red, White and Blue Front on Catharine Street. Will buy anything Farmers have to sell . . . A.G. Shaw."[4] By 1888 his establishment was known as Shaw's Emporium, selling everything the farmer would buy.[5]

1. W. S. Harwood, "The Trans-Mississippi Exposition," *Harper's Weekly*, June 18, 1898, 3–5.
2. Ibid., 3.
3. On the top border, "Ladies Aid Society of the Methodist Episcopal Church," and on the bottom, "Valentine Cherry County."
4. Valentine's merchants seemed partial to colorful storefronts. In addition to Shaw's "Red, White and Blue Front", there was a "White Front," a "Red Front," a "Green Front," and a "Blue Front" along Valentine's commercial streets. Olive Van Metre, *North Country*, vol. 1, *The Old Town: 1880–1889* (self-published, 1977), 118.
5. Biographical data on Amberson Gary Shaw is drawn from Olive Van Metre's *Old Town* (see n. 4, above). Her extensive research on Cherry County pioneers is based in large part on local newspapers from 1883 to 1905, and Shaw's name is a constant figure on their pages. Additional information is found throughout Marianne Brinda Beel, ed., *A Sandhill Century, Book I, The Land—A History of Cherry County, Nebraska* (Valentine, NE: Cherry County Centennial Committee, 1986).

OPPOSITE: Fig. 3 *The Trans-Mississippi Exposition Quilt* (detail)

plaster, and horsehair. They were razed almost immediately afterward, but while they stood they won the highest accolades from the 2.5 million visitors who attended from June to November, 1898.

The entire state was swept up in the excitement of "this really quite remarkable fair."[2] In the Sandhills, in the remote northwest corner of Nebraska, the Ladies Aid Society of the Methodist Episcopal Church decided that even the small town of Valentine should participate in the exposition. They submitted for exhibition in the "woman's work" area of the Liberal Arts Building this wonderfully worked quilt celebrating their community and themselves.

Its purpose is confirmed by the inscription on its left and right borders: Trans-Mississippi Exposition 1898.[3]

As with the *Pawnee City Newspaper Quilt* (see p. 74), many of the blocks (cleverly machine embroidered) replicate the style of newspaper advertisements of the period or are signed by groups of individuals, but this quilt's distinguishing features are the buildings. We can find the Methodist Episcopal Church, the post office, the city's banks, and one of its newspapers, *The Republican* (fig. 1), and the storefronts identify the commercial ventures of most of the leading pioneers and civic leaders: Davenport and Thatcher General

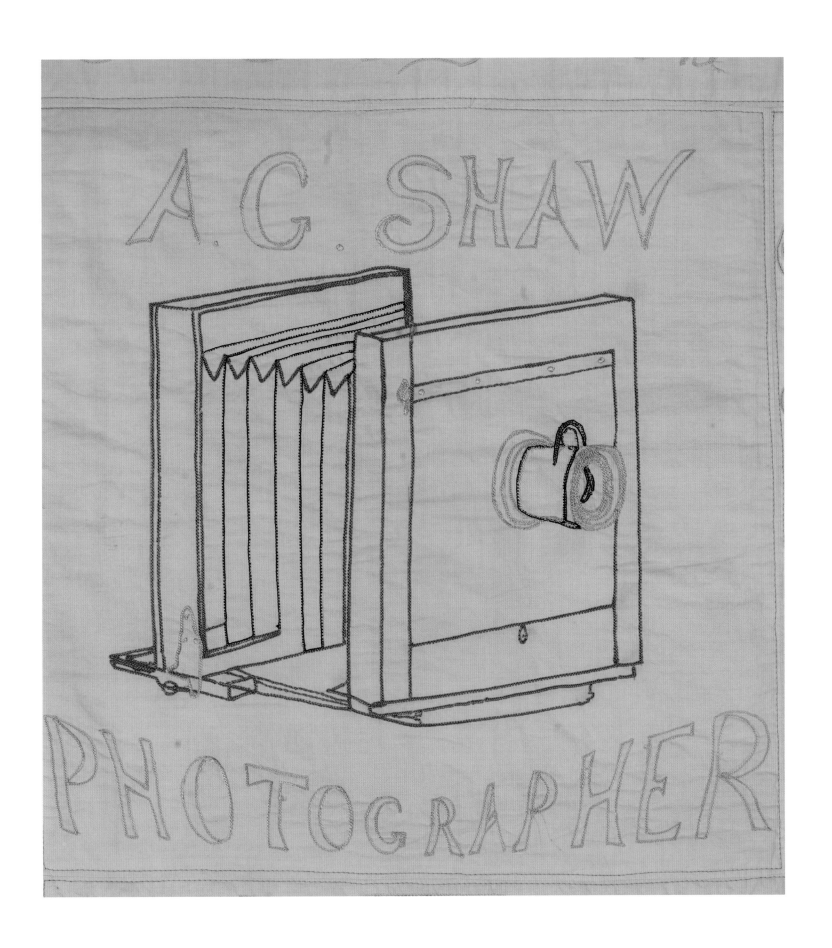

Unfinished Crazy Quilt (reverse)

BRITTA OLSON
Nebraska, late 19th century
TOP: cotton, silk, and velvet; embroidered
REVERSE: flour sacks
59 x 44 (149.9 x 111.8)
Durham Western Heritage Museum, Omaha

Fig. 1 *Unfinished Crazy Quilt (reverse)* (detail)

Although travelers had reached the Pacific Ocean by the middle of the nineteenth century, the trails did not truly close until its end. When the rough jumping-off places along the Missouri had grown into vigorous commercial centers, wagons continued to roll. Even well after the first great rush of overland migration (1840s–50s), particularly on either side of the Great Platte River Road, good land was still to be found and, through the Homestead Act of 1862, claimed. The farms that were established in Nebraska's vast open spaces would help to define the territory and, eventually, the state. In the early years of the Republic the family farm was idealized in Jefferson's concept of agrarian democracy, the inherent goodness and strength of the American farmer; rural Nebraska was formed and sustained by that agrarian theology.

The farmwife was, of course, an integral part of the rural economic unit that was the small Nebraska farm or ranch, and for most it was a hard life indeed. She may well have been a farmwife in the life she had, often reluctantly, left behind, and the work there would have been hard as well, but whereas she had known a comfortable community, crops in the fields, gardens growing, now it was her lot to begin again.

The loss of community was often the most difficult to bear. Away from the population center in eastern Nebraska, the farmwife's existence on a vast, treeless prairie usually was one of dreadful isolation, broken only occasionally by a long wagon or buggy ride to a pioneer wedding, a burying, or, when distance and the weather allowed, to a church gathering or a meeting of a quilt club or sewing circle.

It is unclear as to whether Britta Olson worked this unfinished crazy quilt in a remote rural area or in urban, social surroundings. The piece is without any partic-

ular aesthetic or technical merit, but its unbacked state allows us to see the flour sacks that served as the ground fabric for the embroidery stitches on the quilt's face. Next to a sack's trademark (J. C. HOFF-MAYR & CO. / [ILLEGIBLE] PROCESS / CITY ROLLER MILLS / BEMIS OMAHA BAG CO. / FANCY PATENT) is the most popular and charming of agrarian images, a strutting, crowing rooster (fig. 1). Throughout the nineteenth century, that image appeared on a great variety of surfaces: sheet-iron weather vanes, paper feedbag patterns, political broadsides, a painted political banner (HURRAH FOR GARFIELD & ARTHUR), and among a number of vignettes on an early printed children's handkerchief.[1] Importantly, it is found embroidered large in the very center of a dear, little New Jersey child's quilt.[2]

On the farm, bags held grain, feed, and fertilizer. Replacing wooden boxes, fabric bags were a welcome presence in a woman's kitchen, holding all manner of foodstuffs such as flour, sugar, and salt. The smallest cotton bag held her hus-band's tobacco (or her own!). All could be (and were) recycled into quilts, front and/or back, and clothing—"found fabric" particularly welcome during the Civil War, World War I, and the Great and statewide depressions.

1. The poem beneath the rooster: "the Cock that crowed in the Morn that waked the Priest / all shaven and shorn that married the Man all tattered and torn / that kiffed [kissed] the Maiden all forlorn that milked the Cow with / the crumpled horn that toffed [tossed] the Dog that worried the / Cat that killed the Rat that ate the Malt that lay in the House / that Jack built."

2. Illustrated in Sandi Fox, *Small Endearments: Nineteenth-century Quilts for Children and Dolls*, 2nd ed. (Nashville, TN: Rutledge Hill, 1994), 130–34.

Mary Prokopec's Star Medallion Crazy Quilt

MARIE TEJKL PROKOPEC
Clarkson, Colfax County, Nebraska, about 1900
wool; embroidered
79 x 67¾ (200.7 x 172.1)
Howells Historical Society Museum

The family of Vaclav Tejkl emigrated from Bohemia to Colfax County, Nebraska, in 1879, and it was in that Czechoslovakian community that the Tejkls' daughter Marie married Vincent Prokopec, April 29, 1886, at the age of seventeen. In very modest circumstances they raised eleven children. Marie's quilt was the work of the heart as well as that of the hand: it was worked for Vaclav's brother John and his wife, Josefa, themselves childless, in appreciation for the steady support they had given them in raising their large family.

Colfax County was one of eight counties in the eastern part of the state carved out of Platte County in 1869; those counties would eventually become the center of rural Czech population in the state.[1] Fleeing an 1848 revolution, and lured by the promise of land on either side of the Great Platte River Road, many Czechs immigrated to America, settling in Iowa, Illinois, and later Nebraska.[2] In the small rural areas in which Czech families settled, the Czech culture was carefully protected. Czech was the language of the community, social life centered around the churches, and social clubs strengthened the customs of the Old World. Businesses catered to the ethnic community, and foreign language newspapers flourished.

Immigrant women brought with them, and maintained, many of their exquisite needlework traditions. In Czechoslovakia the tradition of decorated textiles was remarkably rich, but the intricate stitches were primarily displayed on costumes and a variety of household linens: there seems not to have been an extensive tradition of quilts.[3] But near the end of the century, Marie Tejkl Prokopec determined to make a quilt: she chose a style then wildly popular in her new homeland and embellished its rich surface with the same embroidered motifs of flowers and birds she had worked in her girlhood (fig. 1).

1. Butler, Colfax, Cuming, Douglas, Knox, Pawnee, and Saline.
2. For an account of the 1869 overland journey of Czech immigrant Jan Novotny and his family from Linn County, Iowa, see Karel Novotny, "Children, This is That Promised Land," in Vladimir Kucera and Alfred Novacek, eds., *Czech Contributions to the Progress of America* (Lincoln, NE: n.p., 1976), 78.
3. Antonin Vaclavic and Jaroslav Orel, *Textile Folk Art* (London: Spring Books, n.d.), 17.

OVERLEAF: Fig. 1 *Mary Prokopec's Star Medallion Crazy Quilt* (detail)

"Wagon Wheels" with Embroidered Elements

UNIDENTIFIED MAKER
1900; cotton, wool
86½ x 71½ (219.7 x 181.6)
Dawson County Historical Society Museum, Lexington

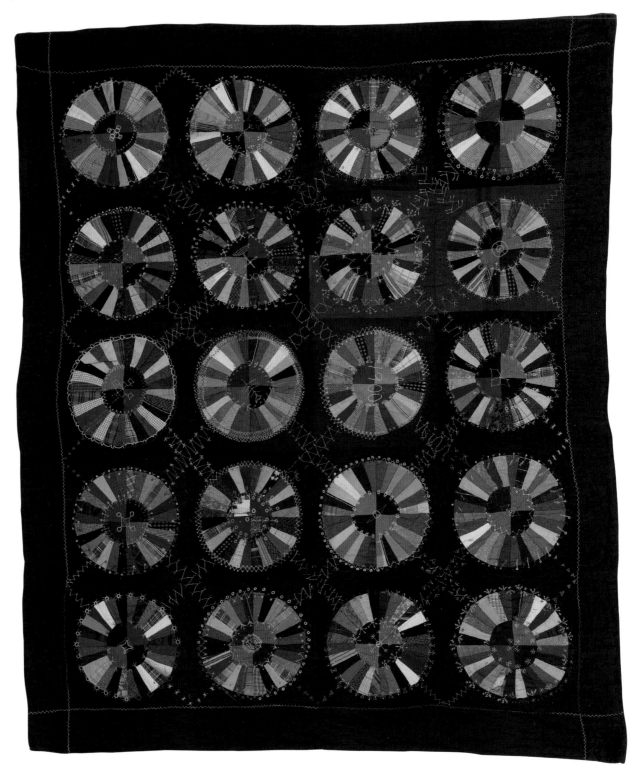

"Wagon Wheels" with Sawtooth Border

MAPLE GROVE SEWING CIRCLE
1907; wool and silk
86¼ x 66 (219.2 x 167.6)
Webster County Historical Museum, Red Cloud, NE, made by the Maple Grove
Sewing Circle and donated by Dorothy and Hazel Miner of Guide Rock, NE, in 1965

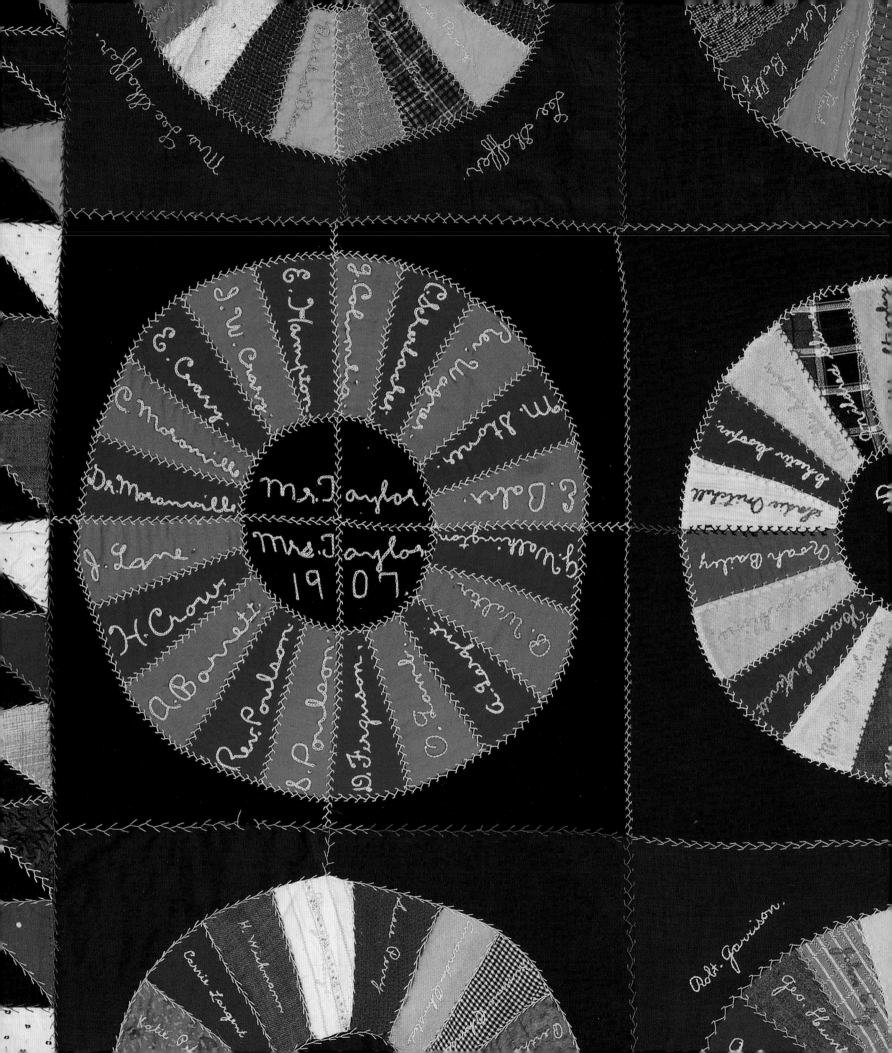

The G.A.R. Shields Quilt

PROBABLY MADE BY THE WOMAN'S RELIEF CORPS
provenance unknown, post–Civil War
cotton; pieced, appliquéd, and quilted; inked signatures
69 x 82 (175.3 x 208.3)
Hastings Museum of Natural and Cultural History

The shield as a military motif enjoyed a surge of popularity following the Spanish American War in 1898; twenty comprise the central field of this faded and deteriorated signature quilt marked GAR, or Grand Army of the Republic, a veterans' organization formed after the Civil War. The quilt had been carefully constructed: tiny white buttonhole stitches applied thirteen stars to each shield and the shield itself to the white ground (fig. 1).

The names are generally illegible, seemingly written by each individual in a variety of inks and with a variety of pens. Their military nature, the various military affiliations following each name (e.g., "Division," "Company," "Cavalry"), and the states represented (Illinois, Nebraska, Iowa, Indiana, New York, Maine, Wisconsin, Vermont, Pennsylvania, and Missouri) strongly suggest that, like the *G.A.R. Flag Quilt* (see p. 82), this quilt was associated with an encampment. But whereas the flag quilt was a carefully tended treasure, the *Shields* eventually reverted to utilitarian usage.

The only clue to this quilt's possible ownership is the inscription "Simon Young Co. D 93, Ill" outlined in tiny running stitches of red thread. Perhaps only coincidentally, the first GAR post was opened in Decatur, Illinois.

The Woman's Relief Corps, auxiliary to the GAR, was established in 1883, and its chapters seem to have undertaken a number of quilting projects. We know from the April 25, 1890 "City Talk" column in *The Telegraph* (Friend, Nebraska) that "The Woman's Relief Corps are making a patchwork quilt which will be presented to the Soldiers' Home at Grand Island." It would seem logical that a chapter would have assumed the organization and execution of this ambitious piece.

The efforts of the GAR eventually culminated in the establishment of Memorial Day, and in addition to projects such as fund-raising quilts it fell to the Woman's Relief Corps to assume responsibility for the holiday's attendant ceremonies. Reports of each of the chapters were presented at the organization's annual convention and printed in the events booklet.

Fig. 1 *The G.A.R. Shields Quilt (detail)*

In Nebraska, the first annual convention was held in St. Paul from April 2 through April 4, 1884. That year's booklet and many subsequent issues are in the Nebraska State Historical Society Library; scattered throughout are numerous reports of each corps' Memorial Day activities for the preceding year.[1] Among the activities in 1889:

Kit Carson Corps #43, Albion
Miss Scott sent three beautiful bouquets, to be placed upon the monument for the unknown dead, in memory of her three brothers whose graves are unknown.

Robert McCook Corps #49, Ashland
We attended the services on Memorial Day as a body, and one of the largest gatherings ever had in the town. A very beautiful and touching incident occurred during the exercises. A brave ex-Confederate officer presented a beautiful floral monument with the inscription, "In Honor of Those who Wore the Blue; from One who Wore the Gray."[2]

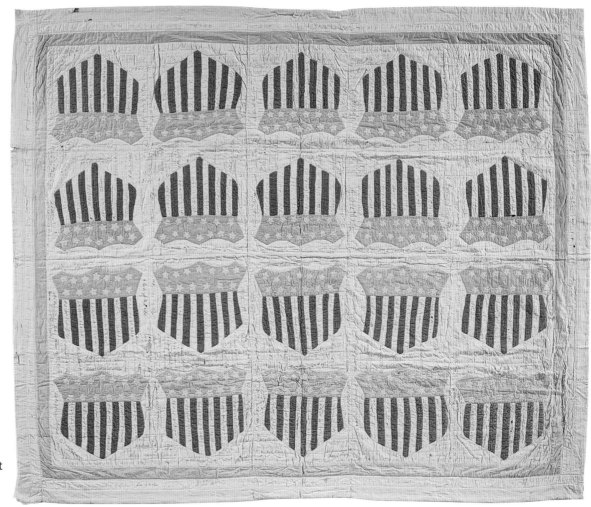

1. I am extremely grateful to David Wells, GAR historian, particularly for directing me to relevant information regarding the Woman's Relief Corps.
2. *Journal of the Seventh Annual Convention of the Department of Nebraska Woman's Relief Corps, Auxiliary to the Grand Army of the Republic, Held at Grand Island, Neb., February 19th and 20th, 1890* (Lincoln, NE: State Journal Co., Printers, 1890), 39, 40.

The Red Cross Quilt

UNIDENTIFIED MAKERS
probably Merrick County, Nebraska, about 1917
cotton; pieced and quilted; inked signatures
75 x 68¼ (190.5 x 173.4)
Merrick County Historical Museum, Central City

While the Woman's Relief Corps continued to honor the veterans of the Civil War, support for a new war, a world war, was added to their patriotic endeavors. Nebraska's Decatur Chapter No. 216 presented a flag to the city, contributed fifty dollars to assist in the purchase of an ambulance for overseas, and, most significantly, committed to raising funds for the Burt County Chapter of the American Red Cross.

They are entitled to the credit of being the originators of the movement for the local Red Cross auction sale, which netted the Red Cross $4,863.57. The Decatur Woman's Relief Corps made 20 quilts, which were sold at that auction sale April 3, 1918, for almost $1,000.[1]

Participation in the war effort was urged upon American women by influential ladies' magazines such as *Harper's Bazaar* and *Ladies' Home Journal*. A Red Cross fund-raising quilt was illustrated in the December 1917 issue of the *Modern Priscilla*, and such quilts soon appeared across the country. All were similar in their choice

of the Red Cross as a repetitive motif, but with slight variations in placement and workmanship. Quiltmakers in Merrick County, Nebraska, where this quilt was probably made, distinguished their Red Cross quilt with finely quilted patterns of feathered plumes and wreaths (fig. 1).

Women's patriotism also could be realized in association with the county chapters of the Red Cross, particularly through the activities of each small community's branch. In popular posters of the period, President Woodrow Wilson himself summoned women to "Comradeship in the Red Cross"; volunteers in Fillmore County, wearing the Red Cross on caps and shoulders and delighting in the comradeship the president had offered, answered the call.

The exemplary organization of the Burt County Chapter, for example, led to county-wide community support for all facets of its efforts; local organizations, secular and religious, supported its fund-raising events, and almost every woman joined the work parties in the local rooms given over to the Red Cross—and why

would they not, when the "Boys Over There" were their boys, their own sons and husbands and fathers?[2]

War efforts had always benefited from the work of women's hands, and the Great War (as World War I was also called) was no exception. Sewing machines and materials were set up in school gymnasiums, Masonic Halls and courthouses; in Oakland, volunteers donned caps and aprons three days a week, and assembled lint and gauze into surgical dressings in the rear of the Farmers and Merchants National Bank. The sewing rooms were usually open every afternoon except Sunday; quotas were assigned and seemingly always met.

Throughout Burt County, women cut out and assembled hospital garments for the soldiers, pieced quilts, and cut material for gas masks to be assembled by schoolchildren. And everywhere, everyone picked up their knitting needles. Knitting was a favored activity for most elderly women who could work in their homes and who would have recalled the vast number of

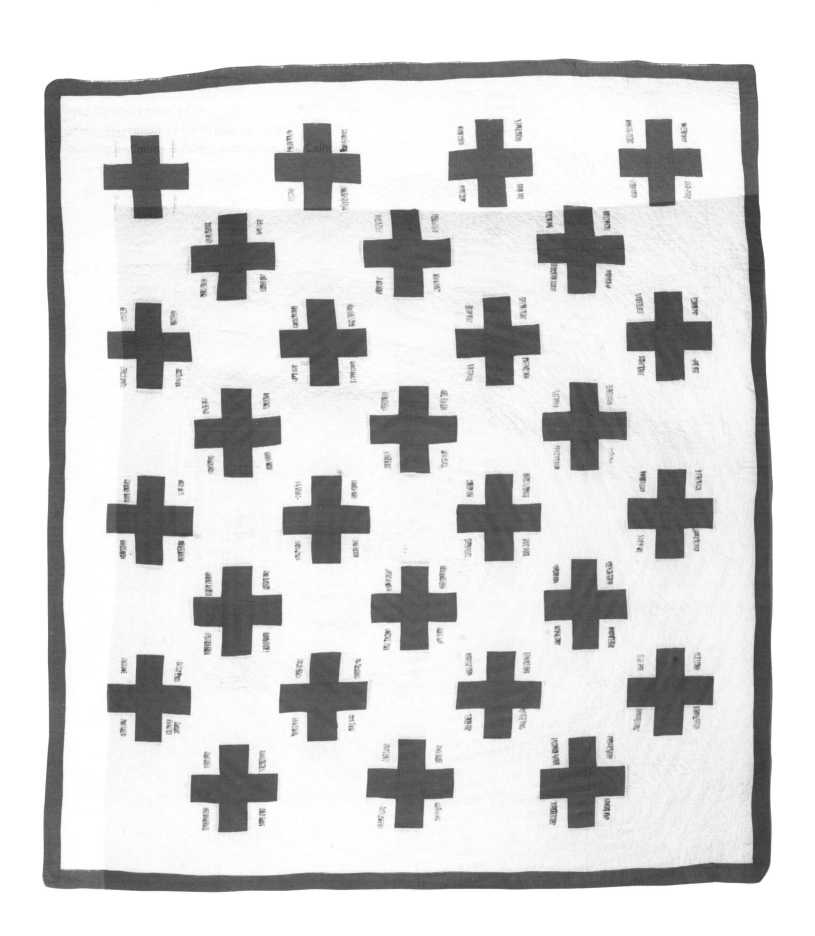

Fig. 1 *The Red Cross Quilt* (detail)

knitted articles they worked for both Union and Confederate soldiers during the Civil War. Women knitted on trains and at parties; their socks and sweaters, mufflers and caps and wristlets would keep the soldiers warm.

Raising funds for the purchase of supplies and other activities required continuous fund-raising efforts, and the manner in which this was accomplished was both inventive and (particularly in Burt County) overwhelmingly successful. Events such as box socials, community dinners, and lectures raised substantial funds, but the auction sales first suggested by the Woman's Relief Corps developed into the most successful vehicle of all. Quilts continued to be offered (one worked by "girl patriots" brought $1,256 in a Tekamah auction), but the contents of the sales expanded to all manner of goods. In support of the war effort it seemed there would be bids on everything, and most items sold well above their real value. At another Woman's Relief Corps benefit, an auction sale and dinner in Decatur:

. . . a pair of hens given by Mrs. Albert Castor were dressed in the national colors by Mrs. Parker, sold at Dutch auction for $199.50; two eggs laid by these hens brought $9.50; the squeal of a pig sold for $3.50; the crow of a rooster $3.00; a Red Cross quilt made by the pupils of Miss Hessie Best sold for $520, and a silk quilt made by High School pupils brought over $400. Eighteen quilts made and donated by the Woman's Relief Corps brought almost $1,000; a pair of ducks sold for $79.[3]

1. *Victory: Burt County Nebraska in the World War* (Tekamah, NE: The Burt County Herald, 1919), 104. This extensively detailed and illustrated publication contains reports of the fund-raising and work activities of each of the Burt County Chapter auxiliaries: Bertha, Craig, Decatur, Lyons, Oakland, and Tekamah.

2. In proportion to its population, Nebraska sent to war more soldiers and sailors than any other state; 840 were from Burt County.

3. *Victory: Burt County Nebraska in the World War*, 89.

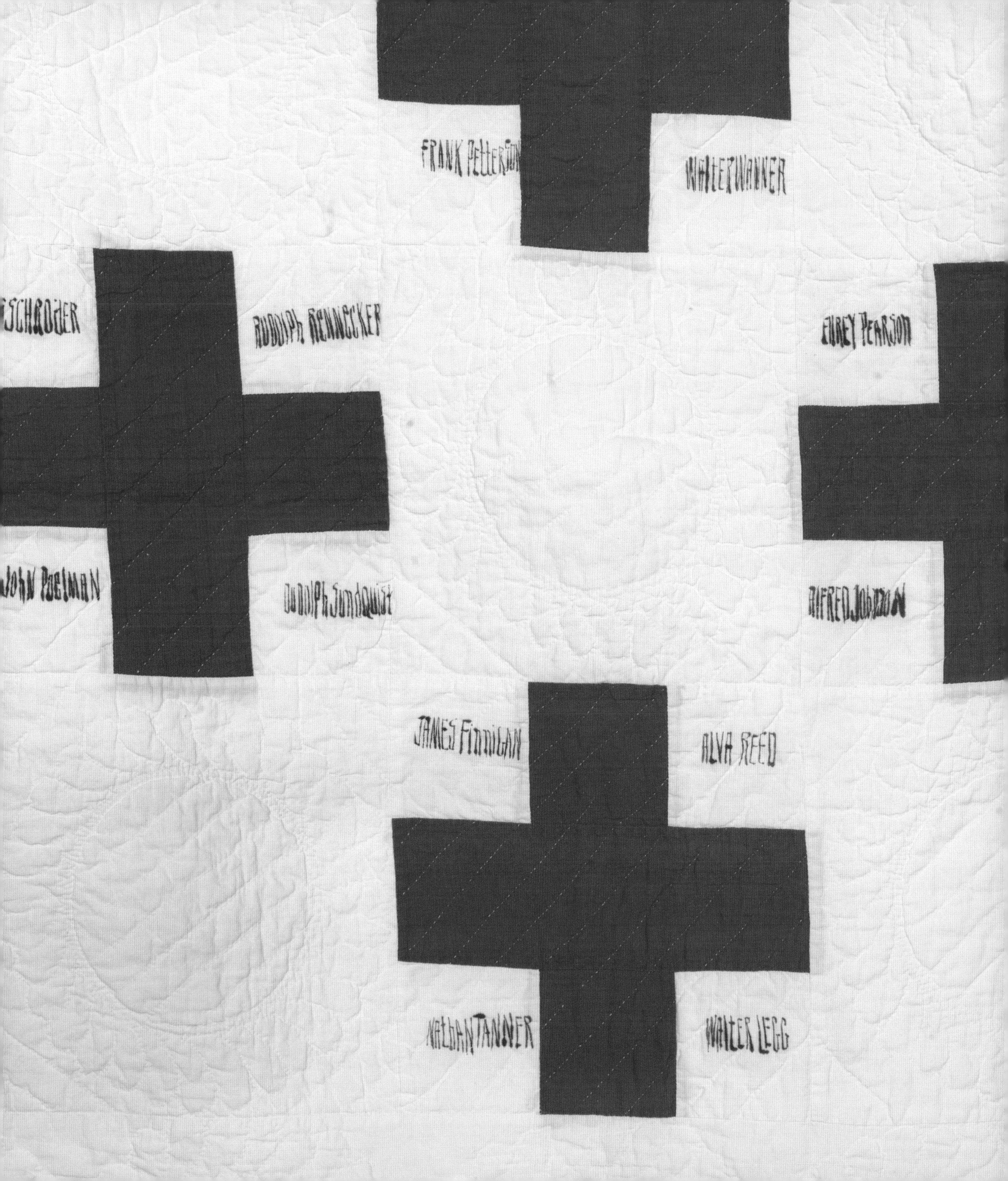
FRANK PETTERSON
WALTER WANNER
SCHRODER
RUDOLPH RENNECKER
ELREY PEARSON
JOHN POELMAN
UDOLPH SUNDQUIST
ALFRED JOHNSON
JAMES FINNIGAN
ALVA REED
NATHAN TANNER
WALTER LEGG

Thirty Blocks, Crazy Quilt

ANNA AND RUTH NELSON
1900; wool
78 x 70 (198.1 x 177.8)
Plainsman Museum, Aurora

Circles with Points and Multiple Signatures

UNIDENTIFIED MAKER
about 1905; cotton
84 ½ x 80 (214.6 x 203.2)
Nebraska Prairie Museum of the Phelps County Historical Society, Holdrege

The Grand Island Pioneer's Reunion Quilt

UNIDENTIFIED MAKER
1907; cotton
66½ x 69 (168.9 x 175.3)
Stuhr Museum of the Prairie Pioneer, Grand Island

Fans with Embroidered Floral Sprays

UNIDENTIFIED MAKER
about 1908; cotton, wool
90 x 78 (228.6 x 198.1)
Clay County Museum, Clay Center

Embroidered Wool Bedcover

MRS. KEN ARMBRUSTER
York, York County, Nebraska, 1904
wool; embroidered
84 ½ x 69 ½ (214.6 x 176.5)
Anna Bemis Palmer Museum, York

Embroidered Wool Bedcover (detail)

Leaving Fort Kearney, Rebecca Ketcham and her company set their course up the Platte River. As she wrote in her 1853 journal: "Yesterday we came in sight of the river. They think it a mile wide." She seemed equally impressed with her latest botanical find: "Today we found a new and beautiful flower, a tall stalk with delicate purple flower."[1]

Many of these botanical notes focus only and, as did Rebecca's, often briefly, on the new and the unidentifiable. Others recorded their floral impressions more simply and sweetly. Harriet Talcott Buckingham celebrated her nineteenth birthday on the trail from Ohio to Oregon with her aunt and uncle in 1851:

Crossed the Missouri. The Pararie is covered with beautiful little flowers. Whose fragrance surpassed any garden flowers. There is a modest little white flower which peeps up among the green grass. Which particularly strikes my fancy. I call it the Pararie Flower. Autumn sun will bring the more gorgeous flowers.[2]

Fifty years later, at the beginning of another century, it was a similar sweetness and simplicity that Mrs. Ken Armbruster (then a girl of twelve) embroidered onto the thirty-five floral panels of this woolen bedcover. The pattern is unidentified; it was perhaps a commercial pattern or one glimpsed in one of the popular women's magazines, or drawn by an indulgent family member or neighbor.

The designs differ primarily in the modest variety of leaves, but they are embellished with a variety of carefully worked embroidery stitches. The stylized flowers and leaves are constructed in chain and herringbone stitches; they bloom on a featherstitched stem above a two-handled basket. Once the last block was finished, all were joined with seams and then embellished with a neat little variation of the featherstitch. The piece was then backed (as were many wool quilts of the period) with plaid cotton flannel.

This charming textile evokes certain stylistic preferences of many colonial American needleworkers. A number of extant embroidered bedcovers (some in wool, others in linen) present similar images on usually smaller blocks. In what must have been an exercise in patience for a young girl, this piece carried the threads of early American embroidered bedcovers into a third century.

1. Leo M. Kaiser, ed., "From Ithaca to Clatsop Plaines, Miss Ketcham's Journal of Travel," *Oregon Historical Quarterly* (1961): 274.
2. Kenneth L. Holmes, ed., "The Diary of Harriet Talcott Buckingham," *Covered Wagon Women: Diaries & Letters from the Western Trails, 1840–1890*, vol. 3 (Glendale, CA: Arthur H. Clark, 1984), 22.

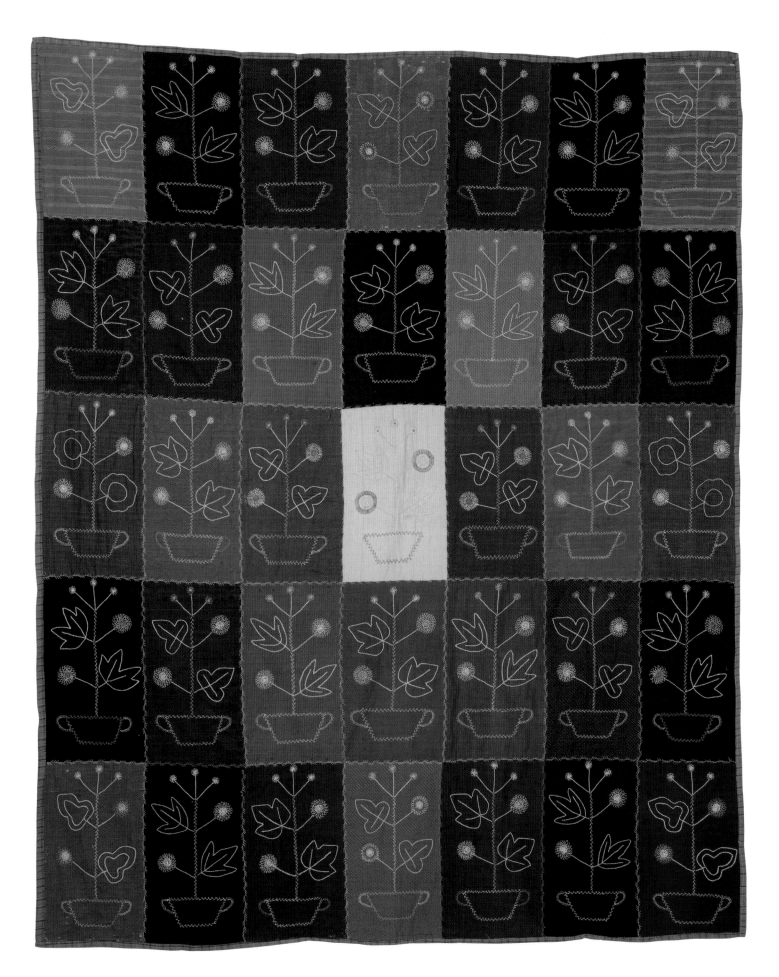

The Bemis Bag Comforter

UNIDENTIFIED MAKER
probably Omaha, Douglas County, Nebraska, about 1908
cotton and silk; pieced and embroidered
82 x 60¾ (208.3 x 154.3)
Douglas County Historical Society, General Crook House Museum, Omaha

Fig. 1 *The Bemis Bag Comforter* (detail)

Single girls went west in notable numbers, often without their families. Some traveled with a small company from their town or village, often without a specific protector. Others earned their way by being of assistance to the wife in the family in whose wagon she traveled. Such was the case with Mormon overlander Ruth Page Rogers, who packed her few "worley goods" to travel with Mr. and Mrs. Wallace Raymond in June 1852: "The agreement was, that I was to do the washing ironing and cooking for six persons and nurse his wife in her confinement."[1]

Like many young women, Ruth went west for her religion; others saw an improved prospect of matrimony at the end of the trail. But for many, financial independence was the primary inducement for undertaking that arduous and hazardous journey. Where did they find the courage and the confidence to face what lay ahead?

For those who sought a modest economic future for themselves, a measure of that confidence may well have come

from the examples set by the young factory girls in the textile mills of Lowell, Massachusetts.[2] Drawn from rural Maine, Massachusetts, New Hampshire, and Vermont, the mill girls made up seventy-five percent of the workers. The work was hard but no more so than the physical work they had provided, unpaid, on the family farm. Although less than men's, their salaries were considerably more than what they would have earned for domestic work and were the highest wages of female employees anywhere in the country.

Most importantly, the mill girls were independent, enjoying for the first time the fruits of their labor. They could assist their families or educate a brother, but the decision to spend their wages on others was theirs. They could purchase bits of finery and sweets, and buy books. Most maintained savings accounts. They considered themselves a cut above other mill girls, and so it would seem they were.

These New England farm girls were healthy, virtuous, and simply educated. Their employer, Boston Associates, estab-

lished a system of subsidized but mandatory boardinghouses whose many detailed regulations and watchful housemothers (responsible to the company) sought to protect and foster the qualities for which these girls had been recruited. Boardinghouse keepers were responsible for seeing to it that the girls were vaccinated (at company expense), that curfews were enforced and improper behavior reported, and that attendance at public worship was observed. Attention was paid to their social and cultural development. Most mill girls had a common school education, and illiteracy was almost unknown; many had left the poorly paid position of rural schoolteacher. In their leisure time, in addition to sewing dresses for themselves and quilt-

112

ing, they read novels and attended lectures in Lowell.

In Omaha, Nebraska, a half-century later, another textile manufacturer adopted a similarly progressive approach to the welfare and comfort of its workforce. The Bemis Omaha Bag Company set up a factory in Omaha in the spring of 1887, manufacturing burlap and cotton bags and selling their wares from the Missouri to the Pacific.[3] Articles in the *Omaha Bee* speak of community support for the Bemis factory girls: "The young women of the Bemis Bag factory were very pleasantly entertained by the Young Women's Christian association . . . to promote and stimulate sociability among the girls."[4]

One would hope those experiments in sociability at least occasionally included quiltmaking, but we cannot know if this comforter was constructed by those working hands. Obviously the design of the bags from which these calendar pages were cut (two months per panel) was a clever inducement for domestic purchase, almost irrespective of what the bags contained. The individual panels were bordered in blue and sashed, and the border embellished with embroidery. The assembled panels were joined to a backing, then tied at intervals with three strands of colored thread.

One panel features scant stitchery, with the turkey slung over a pilgrim's shoulder worked in outline stitch and the holly additionally embellished. Although the panels do not appear in chronological order, two complete series are included, those printed in 1906 and 1907. In 1906, lush floral sprays support the double calendar pages: roses and buds, violets, carnations, sweet peas, mums, and poppies. In 1907, scenic

and figurative elements appear: a New Year baby and signs of the Zodiac (fig. 1), a mill with waterwheel, an Indian woman paddling a canoe, a hay wagon drawn by two horses and three men with pitchforks, and a hunter with rifle and hounds—all popular, illustrated motifs of the period.

1. The Rogers journal (108 pages, unpaginated) is preserved in the collection of the Latter-day Saints Church Archives, MS 1854.

2. The principal source of information on the Lowell mills and the young women who operated their looms is Benita Eisler, ed., *The Lowell Offering: Writings by New England Mill Women (1840–1845)* (Philadelphia: J. P. Lippincott, 1977).

3. James W. Savage, John T. Bell, and Consul W. Butterfield, *History of the City of Omaha, Nebraska, and South Omaha* (New York, Chicago: Munsell, 1894), 503.

4. *Omaha Bee*, March 3, 1901, in the collection of the Historical Society of Douglas County, Library/Archives Center, Omaha, Nebraska.

The Milliner's Quilt

MRS. AZUBA READ
Phelps County, Nebraska, about 1910
wool, velvet, silk, cotton, felt, feathers, metal; embroidered
73 x 71 (185.4 x 180.3)
Nebraska Prairie Museum of the Phelps County Historical Society, Holdrege

The milliner's shop was an early presence on the streets of frontier towns—the settlers' wives demanded it! They had given up almost everything to accommodate this move to the prairie, but they were not prepared to give up fashion.

A great number of practical occupations were open to women in the West, from boardinghouse operator to postmistress. Even in the early days of settlement there was a demand for milliners and dressmakers; in Nebraska, the Ninth Census (1870) counted 115 of the former and 57 of the latter.[1] Although many women plied their needles to assist with family finances, others (such as Civil War widows) came west with funds sufficient to establish themselves as the proprietress of their own small shops.

Especially for women in domestic service ("I wonder if I shall always be obliged to drudge"[2]), a milliner must have seemed to have the best of all possible lives: no heavy physical labor, an elevated social status, social contact and conversation with other women, access to fabrics other than the more common calico (with scraps to be retrieved for her own quilts), and a table-top full of *Godey's Lady's Books*, other fashionable women's magazines, and pattern books.

Women in eighteenth-century America devised ways to keep current with what was fashionable in England—letters and sketches from family and friends, small samples and fashion dolls[3]—all to arrive by swift sailing vessels. A century later, women on the frontier required information on the most current fashion in the more civilized East; letters and clippings arrived in similar haste, beginning with the swift horses of the Pony Express. To the extent of the women's funds, these were the fashions they required their milliners and dressmakers to duplicate even on the early and isolated prairies.

Silk, satins and velvets, felt and feathers are featured in abundance on a type of crazy quilt created by Mrs. Azuba Read, a milliner in Phelps County, Nebraska. Born Azuba Kesterson, she married Jesse H. Read on April 1, 1885, in Sidney, Iowa; the couple moved to Nebraska four years later and, with nine children (little Elizabeth died in infancy), eventually to Atlanta, Nebraska, where they converted to Methodism. Phelps County directories list J. H. as the manager of a cream station and Azuba as a milliner.

Perhaps including individual leaves and petals from an eastern source of milliner's supplies, Azuba's clever hands cut and constructed the significant number of embellished botanical elements randomly affixed to this dark ground. The edges and petals of the lovely silk and velvet flowers are often gently tipped with a light wash of a slightly darker tone, their centers embroidered with French knots (fig. 1). Additional applied images are those often found on crazy quilts: an owl, a gloved hand (fig. 2), scattered and sparsely embroidered floral and geometric images, bits of ribbon and miscellaneous pieces of silk, and small silver wire formed into almost illegible script appearing to read "M. Carolina." The piece is completed with a two-inch edging of rather garish multicolored filet crochet.

We do not know exactly where Azuba practiced her trade. Some milliners established their enterprises in a storefront on Main Street, just off the wooden sidewalk, while others established themselves in more modest surroundings that would serve as both shop and home.

1. Ninth Census, 1:692–95, cited in Glenda Riley, *The Female Frontier: A Comparative View of Women on the Prairie and the Plains* (Lawrence: University of Kansas Press, 1988), 129.
2. Ibid., 128.
3. Linda Baumgarten, *Eighteenth-century Clothing at Williamsburg* (Williamsburg, VA: Colonial Williamsburg Foundation, 1986), 14.

Fig. 1 *The Milliner's Quilt* (detail)

Fig. 2 *The Milliner's Quilt* (detail)

Diamonds on a Crazy Quilt Ground

UNIDENTIFIED MAKER
1917; wool, velvet
82 x 82 (208.3 x 208.3)
Rock County Historical Society Museum, Bassett

Stars and Signatures

UNIDENTIFIED MAKER
1927; cotton
95 x 70 (241.3 x 177.8)
Custer County Historical Society, Broken Bow

Pieced, Appliquéd, and Embroidered Map Panel

WILLIAM C. HODGE
about 1930; cotton
32 x 77 (81.3 x 195.6)
Nebraska Prairie Museum of the Phelps County Historical Society, Holdrege

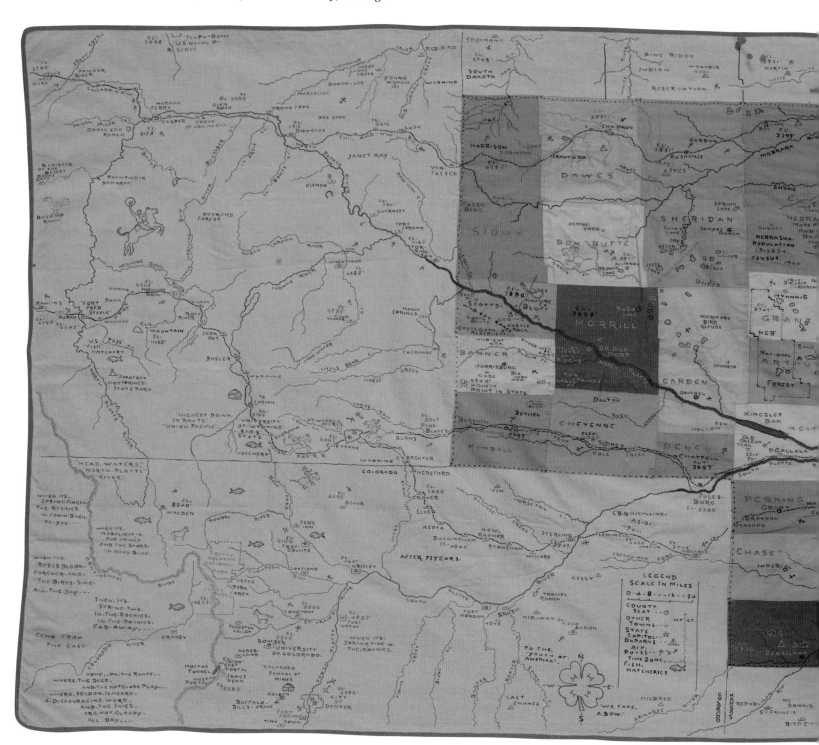

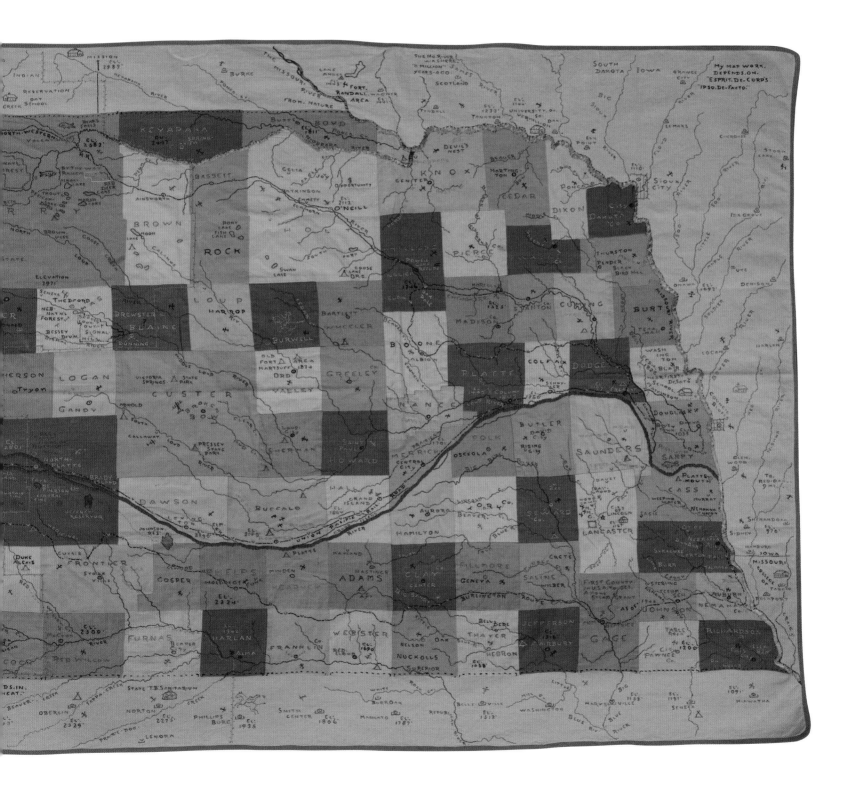

Log Cabin, "Courthouse Steps" Variation with Chevron Border

ATTRIBUTED TO MARY SLABY KRALIK

about 1930–40; cotton

78 ½ x 59 ½ (199.4 x 151.1)

Webster County Historical Museum, Red Cloud, NE, made by

Mary Slaby Kralik and donated by Robert Beardslee of Red Cloud, NE, in 1991

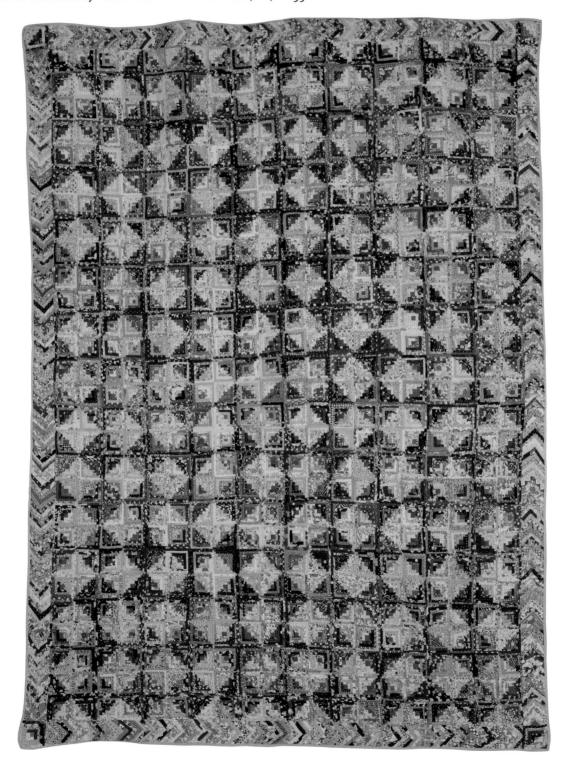

The Comics Quilt

BERNICE ELLIS LUNDER
probably Omaha, Nebraska, 1935
cotton; appliquéd, embroidered, and quilted
78⅜ x 66 (199.1 x 167.6)
Stuhr Museum of the Prairie Pioneer, Grand Island

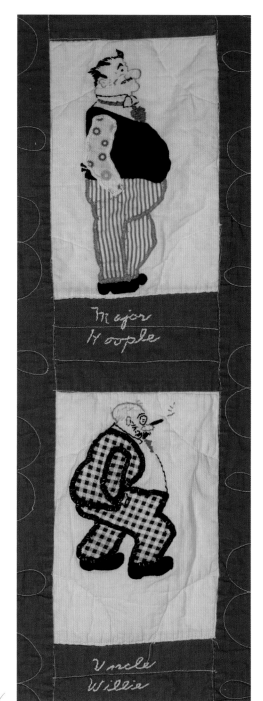

If one did not enjoy the professional status of a milliner or a dressmaker, a woman's dexterity with her needle and thread could nevertheless realize a small amount of "pin money" (and the possibility of a certain notoriety among her community of quilt-makers) through a newspaper or magazine contest, or a state or local fair.

One of the unique quilts that has been entered [in the quilt contest] is one featuring 40 [actually, 49] comic characters. It was made by Mrs. Bernice Lunder . . . Mrs. Lunder drew all the characters free hand and then appliquéd them. Each comic folk is true to character. She spent a year on the pieces and then [machine] quilted it during the last three weeks. It was one of her hobbies as she traveled through western Nebraska with her husband.[1]

The characters' names of this figurative quilt are embroidered in white beneath each of the seven-by-five-inch blocks—all familiar friends from the funny papers. Among the characters are Major Hoople and Uncle Willie (fig. 1); Jiggs and Maggie (fig. 2), the humorous marrieds of George McManus's cartoon strip *Bringing Up Father*; and heavyweight boxing champion Joe Palooka (fig. 3), created by cartoonist Ham Fisher. Other beloved characters include Buttercup, Wimpy, Popeye and Olive Oyle, and Mushmouth.

1. From a clipping in the archives of Omaha's *Evening World Herald*, August 29, 1935.

Fig. 1 *The Comics Quilt* (detail)

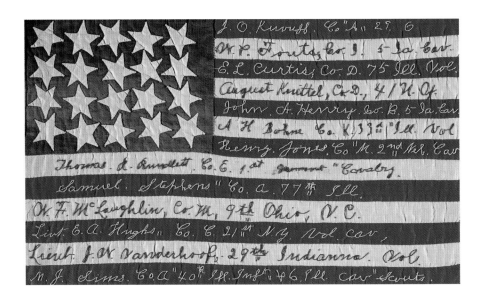

Going West! Quilts and Community

Published in 2007 by the
Smithsonian American Art Museum
in association with
D Giles Limited

Designed by Carol Beehler
Typeset in Quadraat and Quadraat Sans
Printed by Artegrafica, Verona, Italy
on Burgo Larius matt satin

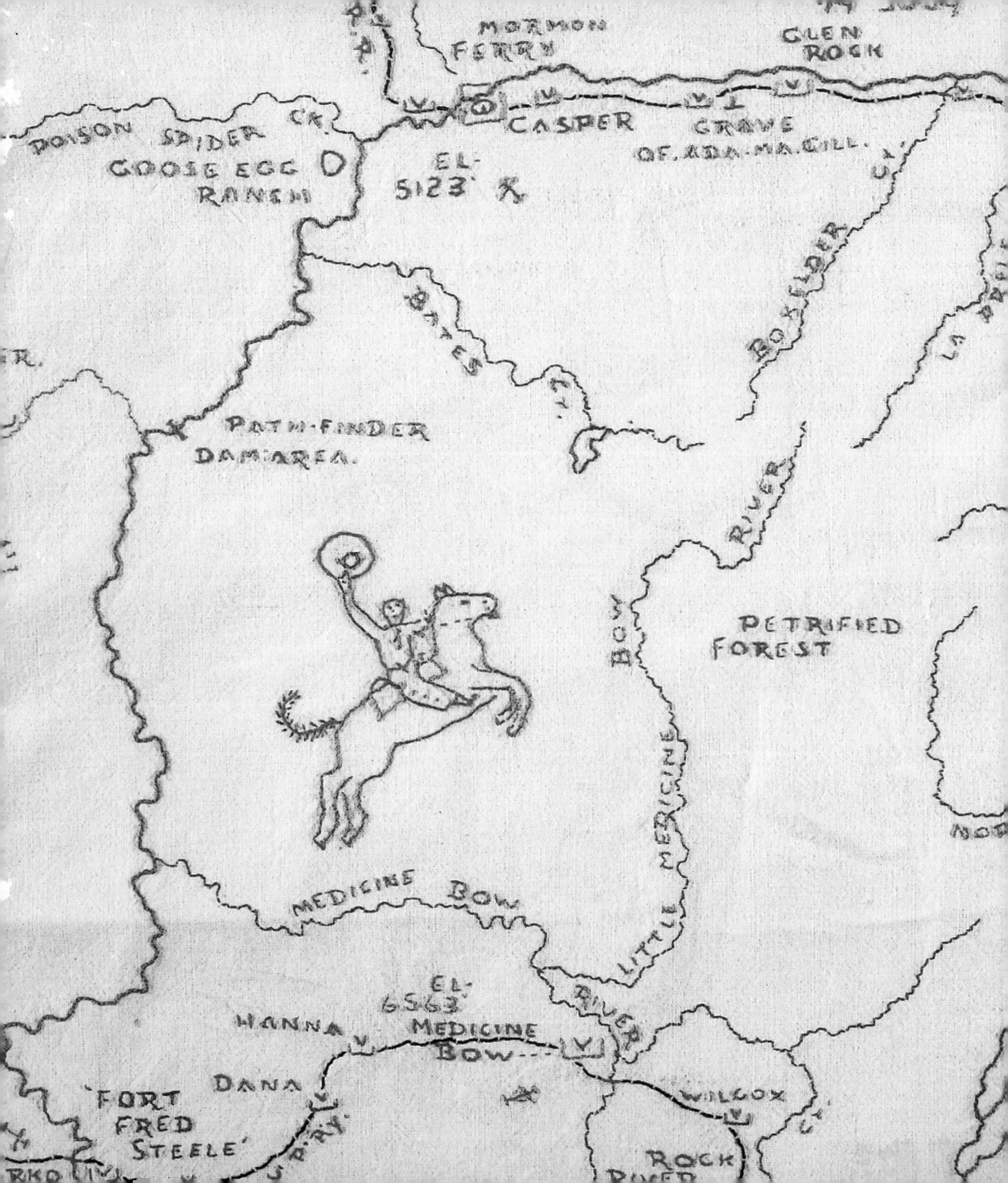
MORMON FERRY
GLEN ROCK
CASPER
GRAVE OF ADA MAGILL
POISON SPIDER CK.
GOOSE EGG RANCH
EL. 5123'
BATES CK.
BOXELDER CK.
PATH-FINDER DAM AREA
BOW RIVER
PETRIFIED FOREST
LITTLE MEDICINE
MEDICINE BOW
EL. 6563'
HANNA
MEDICINE BOW
RIVER
DANA
FORT FRED STEELE
U.P.RY.
WILCOX
CK.
ROCK RIVER